Praise for *The Physic*

Dr. Jose Norberto, an accomplished cardiovascular surgeon, has written an interesting treatise on the crucifixion of Jesus Christ from a physician-surgeon perspective. Readers will find his observations thought-provoking. His unique insights into the aspect of the unbelievable trauma to the human body of Jesus, as reported in Scripture, and his thoughts about the Resurrection, are worth the reader's consideration and attention.

G.B. SNIDER, MD, FACP

Dr. Norberto, a distinguished cardiothoracic surgeon, illustrates in simple words that science and religion are not in contradiction. He is able to create a safe bridge between the religious and the scientific interpretations of Jesus' crucifixion. Reading this book has given me a different perspective about Jesus' life, crucifixion, and resurrection. Dr. Norberto has touched my heart, without being my doctor, and motivated me to continue reading and learning about the real world of Jesus Christ.

CARMEN LAZALA, MD, FAAP

The Physical Death & Resurrection
A Surgeon's View

Dr. Jose J. Norberto

THE PHYSICAL DEATH & RESURRECTION
A Surgeon's View
Copyright © 2014 by Dr. Jose J. Norberto

Scripture quotations are from the Holy Bible, New International Version®, NIV® Copyright © 1973, 1978, 1984, 2011 by Biblica, Inc.® Used by permission. All rights reserved worldwide. Some Scripture quotations have been taken from the Holy Bible, New International Version, copyright 1973, 1978, 1984 by International Bible Society. Used by permission of Zondervan Publishing House. All rights reserved.

Published by Deep River Books
PO Box 310
Sisters, Oregon 97759
www.deepriverbooks.com

ISBN-13: 9781940269146
ISBN-10: 1940269148

Library of Congress: 2014941262

Cover design by Juanita Dix

DEDICATION

This book is dedicated to my parents, Reyes and Gradia, who emphasized the Christian faith as the center of our family life. They never gave up on me during my years away from worship.

To my two daughters, Christina and Jackie, who are such a special present from God to me. They followed with enthusiasm the progress of this book.

My special thanks to our Lord who has given me so many gifts. It has been such a privilege to engage in a project like this. I have enjoyed the journey and his guidance in this endeavor.

CONTENTS

ACKNOWLEDGMENTS

Special thanks to Janessa Castle, who performed such a delicate job in the initial editing of the manuscript. Since the first conversation about this book, she was able to capture my passion for it and was capable to keep it as an integral part of the manuscript. Also, many thanks to Kathryn Deering, whose editorial touch took it to another level.

I would also like to thank Devon Marshall for his fine graphics and illustrations for this enterprise. Thanks to all of you, my team, for your dedication, support, and friendship.

FOREWORD
by Dr. Margaret Sawyer

My first encounter with Dr. Jose Norberto was on my cardiothoracic (CT) surgery rotation as a general surgery intern. The first year of general surgery residency is quite an impressionable year. No longer a medical student, the responsibility of saving people's lives rests solely in your hands. This job, as a general surgery intern, is completely overwhelming and exhilarating at the same time. You can no longer hide behind the veil of being a student. For the first time, you are in charge. It is a very steep learning curve and you must learn from every experience.

Early on in my CT rotation, I met Dr. Norberto at a morbidity and mortality conference. At this conference, the attending physicians discuss the lessons of various cases and learn from each other's experiences. Although Dr. Norberto was a surgeon at a community hospital rather than the typical large academic hospital, he commanded himself as a confident leader and was well-spoken, and I endeavored to learn from him as much as possible.

Over the years, I have come to know him much better, as we practice in the same community hospital. I now realize why he stood apart from the rest. Despite many years of rigorous schedules and challenging surgeries, and countless hours in the operating room every week saving people's lives, Dr. Norberto remains deeply rooted in his strong Christian faith.

After lecturing on the subject of the physical death of Jesus and intensely studying the crucifixion, he writes here about the actual science behind it. And through his efforts, we are offered an opportunity to reflect on our own faith. As physicians, we embark on a lifelong journey to find answers for many of life's toughest questions. When a patient comes to us with a problem, we are responsible for finding the solution. Our scientific background and medical training have ingrained in us a drive to search until the answer is found. This training can create the potential for conflict on the topic of religion. Scientists and physicians may feel troubled by the concept of faith and be reluctant to accept religion. Dr. Norberto has embraced the mysteries of faith, and launched a medical investigation into certain biblical teachings.

The Physical Death and Resurrection takes you on a scientific journey to the time of Christ. Beginning with the Shroud of Turin, Dr. Norberto explores the scientific evidence that links the Shroud to Jesus. In the second section, Dr. Norberto presents an intriguing scientific explanation of the Crucifixion and the Resurrection. The presentation is thoroughly researched and well written, offering its readers the historical and scientific evidence to support the Resurrection. But, in the end, Dr. Norberto's citation to Saint Thomas Aquinas sums it up:

To one who has faith, no explanation is necessary.

To one without faith, no explanation is possible.

MARGARET S. SAWYER, MD

INTRODUCTION

The purpose of this book is very simple: to increase the awareness among Christians of the extreme sacrifice of Jesus, but also to stimulate the curiosity among the non-Christians regarding the extraordinary man named Jesus of Nazareth. Most Christians know that Jesus gave his life for them and that he suffered the most painful mode of execution known to man. Because of his death on the cross, we are forgiven of our sins. He took the sin of this world with him at the time of his death.

My purpose is to create a bridge between the religious interpretation of Jesus' death and the actual physical suffering of that human being who for millions of people is the son of God—the Messiah. Understanding the physical suffering gives a more profound value to his sacrifice, which enables us to make a more serious analysis of our own lives, with the goal of making us worthy of his sacrifice.

On the other hand, for some rationalists who emphasize observable facts only, for whom Jesus was just an extraordinary man, perhaps the greatest human being ever, this book is also helpful. This is because it shares details about how that extraordinary leader was capable of dying (by means of a most barbaric method of execution) without giving up his ideals. He was a leader in the truest sense of the word—and this type of leadership is lacking in current times.

My interest regarding the physical death of Jesus started about twenty years ago, when I read a book about the Shroud of Turin, a grave-wrapping in Italy that has the image of a crucified man imprinted on it. The book summarized the research performed in the 1930s by a multidisciplinary group that included a photographer, a physician, and other researchers. I read the book when I was in medical school, and I was intrigued by the many scientific disciplines involved in this investigation. As I mentioned, it was a multidisciplinary team, but I have to admit that most of my attention was caught by the physician on the team, a surgeon. The physician's description of the wounds was fascinating to me. It was also very interesting to see the initial photos of the Shroud, taken with a very primitive camera by an Italian photographer.

After finishing medical school in the Dominican Republic, I came to the United States for my general surgery training, followed by a cardiothoracic surgery fellowship. Surgical residencies are very intense and there is not too much time to think about anything—you just survive. But I do have to say that my interest in the subject remained during those difficult years and beyond. Recently, I came across some medical literature regarding the crucifixion of Jesus. I was surprised about the impact of a crucifixion on a human body. It made me think deeply about the meaning of his death, its implications for the generations to follow, and how it affects my own life.

I am not quite sure how the whole idea of writing a book started. Maybe it was after one of my lectures regarding medical aspects of the crucifixion. I saw the reaction of the Christian public to my presentation. They wanted more. I thought that some nonbelievers would have the same reaction, and that the thirst to learn more about the greatest historical figure might take them to meet the Messiah.

The whole process of writing about Jesus from this perspective has been unique. Prior to describing the crucifixion proceedings, I took a look at all the information available and made a pre-crucifixion medical profile. How was Jesus' physical health? What was his personality? Also, how was he perceived by others? It was important to briefly explore the socio-political atmosphere during Jesus' time. By understanding his personality and his characteristics as a leader, we can comprehend the conflict between the socio-political establishment and Jesus, the young leader. Obviously, the collision between the two opposing forces ended in Jesus' crucifixion. The elimination of a leader has been used for centuries as method to control unwanted trends or movements. This particular maneuver might work depending on multiple factors, including how early in the movement the removal of the leader occurs, how solid the person's ideology is, how long the followers were exposed to the new ideology, and more. In this case, following an initial period of fear after

Jesus' death, we see an extraordinary energy boost to his religious movement. In basic terms, the crucifixion failed to destroy what Jesus started.

I have to admit that including the resurrection of Jesus was not part of my initial idea for this book. I ended up experiencing what other authors have: Sometimes the book has its own mind. The reality is that Jesus' story is incomplete without the resurrection. It has to be discussed regardless of one's theological position. Human history has not registered another phenomenon like what happened after Jesus' death. His religious movement took off to the point that Roman Empire became Christian in a relatively short time. There is no sociological explanation for this phenomenon. Therefore, I dedicated the last portion of this book to discuss what is considered the energy source of Christianity: the Resurrection.

I feel the need to share with humankind, both believers and non-believers, what I have learned regarding the physical death and resurrection of Jesus. My hope is that a process of self-assessment will take place in the life of each person who reads this book, and my goal is to bring everyone closer to the ideal of Jesus, the leader, the Messiah.

My career allows me to physically touch people's hearts. Now, through this book, I hope God touches yours.

CHAPTER 1

THE SHROUD OF TURIN

Joseph of Arimathea, a prominent member of the Council, who was himself waiting for the kingdom of God, went boldly to Pilate and asked for Jesus' body. Pilate was surprised to hear that he was already dead. Summoning the centurion, he asked him if Jesus had already died. When he learned from the centurion that it was so, he gave the body to Joseph. So Joseph bought some linen cloth, took down the body, wrapped it in the linen, and placed it in a tomb cut out of rock. Then he rolled a stone against the entrance of the tomb.

MARK 15:43–46

The Shroud of Turin is the linen that some believe was used to wrap the corpse of Jesus. Others believe it is just a masterful artistic representation of Jesus' dead body. This piece of linen is rectangular in shape, measuring 4.4 meters by 1.1 meters (14.3 feet by 3.7 feet).

It is safe to say that in the history of humanity, there has been no other piece of linen that has been the subject of such an enormous amount of research. It is beyond the scope of this book to solve the mystery of such a controversial artifact. In fact, whole books have been dedicated exclusively to the Shroud of Turin. However, some information concerning this topic is relevant to the main subject of this book. It seems the more research that is done on the Shroud, the more confusing and mysterious it gets.

Controversy even surrounds the dates when it was found. The most accurate document goes back to the mid-1300s, when Geoffrey de

Charny, a French knight, informed Pope Clement that he was in possession of the Shroud. Its location and host changed numerous times before it reached its current location in Turin, Italy.[1]

Through the years the Shroud of Turin has survived numerous fires, leaving behind burn marks on its fibers that have required mending. On special occasions, this relic has been displayed for the public and to researchers. It was in the public viewing of 1898 that an amateur photographer, Secundo Pia, first photographed the Shroud.[2] This Italian photographer had the privilege of taking the first pictures of this mysterious linen. An initial observation of the cloth revealed the delicate silhouette of a human body. (See Fig. 1.) The novice photographer took the photographic plate to the darkroom to develop it. In the darkroom, he witnessed an extraordinary phenomenon—something for which he was not ready. The negative image showed a very distinctive face; the negative was clearer than the blurred silhouette he had just photographed. (See Fig. 2.) After several hours of inspecting the photos, he came to the conclusion that the original Shroud is the actual negative. What source of energy or what event might have created a negative-image silhouette in the Shroud?

In May 1931, the Shroud was displayed again and a second photographer, a professional named Giuseppe Enrie, had the opportunity to photograph the relic. This time, the Shroud was photographed using modern equipment, and in the presence of the pioneer, Mr. Pia. Mr. Enrie confirmed the 1898 findings of Mr. Pia.[3] The formal inspection of the Shroud of Turin had just begun.

Simultaneously, during the public viewing of 1931, a surgeon was assigned to describe the image of the Shroud from a medical point of view. Dr. Pierre Barbet studied the image of the Shroud very closely. He described the wounded dead body as reflected on the Shroud. The graphic description of the image corresponds to a man who had been brutally injured, a man who suffered a form of execution that is not used in modern times: crucifixion.

He performed a very tedious and systematic inspection, followed by a description of his findings. One of the findings that caught his attention was that the nails went through the wrists. He was puzzled by the fact that the nailing did not take place in the palms as described by the Bible or as traditionally described, but rather in the wrists. He needed to analyze his findings, since this contradicted with the traditional historical beliefs. He performed extensive experiments using recently amputated arms in which he passed nails through the palms in one group and through the wrists in a second group, then added 100 pounds of weight. The results were breathtaking: the weight could not be sustained with a nail through the palm, but a wrist was capable of supporting the weight.[4] His experiments confirmed what the Shroud revealed, that crucifixion must have been performed by driving the nails through the wrists rather than the palms.

But then, how could the biblical description, "they pierced my hands and my feet" (Psalm 22:16, KJV) be explained? It was paramount to solve the mystery and explain the discrepancy. Solving the riddle required that Dr. Barbet review the anatomical nomenclature. His conclusion: "Anatomists of every age and land regard the wrist as an integral part of the hand, which consists of the wrist, the metacarpus, and the fingers."[5] In other words, the wrist can legitimately be called "the hand," as it was in that psalm.

It is noteworthy to realize that artwork pertaining to the crucifixion can be divided into two eras: before and after the classic work published by Dr. Barbet. It is not unusual to observe the nails through the palms in old sculptures or paintings created prior to the discovery of this French physician. Most of the recent artwork tends to be more accurate from the anatomical standpoint.

After examining the Shroud, the physician considered that the wounds visible in this image correspond to the methodology used in Roman crucifixion. He also indicated that there were specific injuries on the head that must have been caused by the crown of thorns, as well as a wound in the chest, both of which pointed more specifically to the crucifixion of Jesus as the Bible describes it.

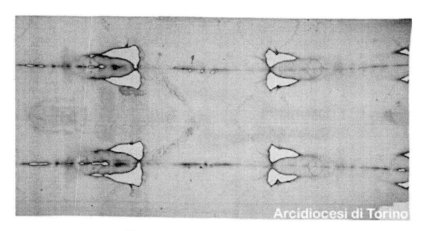

The entire figure on the Shroud

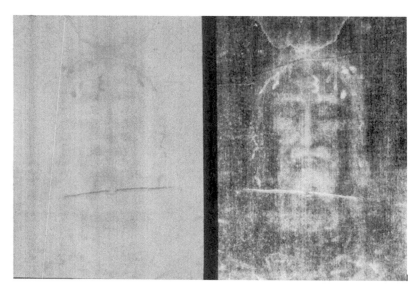

Negative image of the face on the Shroud

[Images used by permission of the Holy Shroud Guild]

RECENT RESEARCH AND CONTROVERSIES

Admittedly, the research concerning the Shroud of Turin is extremely complex. As I mentioned earlier, it is beyond the scope of this book to prove the authenticity of the cloth. Since a lot of the medical knowledge regarding crucifixion as a method of execution was obtained from the work of Dr. Pierre Barbet, it is necessary to discuss some of the issues in more detail.

In my surgical practice, I try to figure out the patient's problems, simplify them, and then establish a reliable, reproducible, uncomplicated plan. It is easier to remember a simple plan than an overwhelming, unnecessarily complex procedure. It is also important when approaching a complex issue to have an organized approach. Just as Jesus used simple language when he taught, I will do the same when explaining the complexities surrounding the Shroud.

In 1976, a group of American scientists at Sandia laboratories in Los Alamos, New Mexico used a very sophisticated image analyzer to study Mr. Enrie's 1931 picture of the Shroud. This image analyzer, which is called the VP-8 Image Analyzer, is utilized to create relief maps from moon photographs and any other topographic map. The principle is to convert lights and darks into shadows and highlights, creating a three-dimensional image. This analyzer created a 3-D image out of the 1931 photo of the Shroud. You might ask why this information is important. Well, a regular photo will not produce a 3-D image. The Shroud has a 3-D code within it, illustrating that a real human being was wrapped in this linen. This particular finding by Dr. John Jackson, Bill Mottern, and others was the starting point for The Shroud of Turin Research Project, also known as STURP.[6] More recently, husband and wife team Ray and Maria Downing were able to create a computer-generated face of Jesus based on the 3-D code of the shroud image. Sophisticated graphic software took the image, plus other variables such as ethnicity and gender, and created a 3-D image of Jesus' face. Their work is searchable online.

STURP is an American multidisciplinary research team that in 1978 conducted 120 hours of consecutive experimentation on the Shroud. They also obtained enough samples for future experiments by them or any other research group. In October 1981, after several years of analysis, the group issued a press conference and gave the following conclusion:

> We can conclude for now that the Shroud image is that of a real human form of a scourged, crucified man. It is not the product of an artist. The blood stains are composed of hemoglobin and also give a positive test for serum albumin. The image is an ongoing mystery and until further chemical studies are made, perhaps by this group of scientists, or perhaps by some scientists in the future, the problem remains unsolved.[7]

Since this particular statement, there have been other interesting developments. Some of the investigations are rather tedious, but I find others very interesting. For instance, I did not realize that pollen identification was used in criminal forensics to establish where an object was previously located. A Swiss criminologist, Max Frei, identified fifty-eight different types of pollen grains that had been trapped in the fabric fibers of the Shroud. These pollens came from plants that grow around the Dead Sea and Negev, central and western Turkey, Constantinople, and western Europe. Max Frei's findings were confirmed by Avinoam Danin, a botany professor at the Hebrew University of Jerusalem, and Uri Baruch, a pollen specialist with the Israel Antiquities. They reported in 1999 that the pollen could come only from the flora growing in a restricted area around Jerusalem.[8]

Even from the earliest pollen studies, it appeared the Shroud was authentic, but one piece of information was missing: the date. The moment to determine the age of the Shroud arrived in 1988, using C-14 or carbon dating, the scientific method used to determine how old an object is. Three different companies obtained sections of the same sample piece of the Shroud. The result was given to the media in a press conference in October 1988. The approximated date was around AD 1325, which obviously puts the authenticity of the linen into question.

On top of that, neither of these research results explains how the human silhouette was formed. By now, you can start to see the scientific web around this piece of cloth. It gets better. A peer-reviewed scientific publication by Raymond Rogers in the journal *Thermochimica Acta* concluded:

> As unlikely as it seems, the sample used to test the age of the Shroud of Turin in 1988 was taken from a rewoven area of the Shroud. Pyrolysis—mass spectrometry results from the sample area coupled with microscopic and microchemical observations prove that the radiocarbon sample was not part of the original cloth of the Shroud of Turin. The radiocarbon date was thus not valid for determining the true age of the Shroud.[9]

It is important to expound on the significance of a peer-reviewed publication. In the scientific world, peer review carries a lot of weight. The scrutiny that an experiment has to go through for publication can be overwhelming. Therefore, credibility is enhanced considerably when the results get published in a peer-reviewed scientific journal.

In basic terms, the sample selected for the carbon date was not part of the original cloth. Most likely it came from one of the multiple mendings the Shroud has gone through. In other words, it was a sampling error, believe it or not.

The Shroud appears to have very old blood stains on it. Scientists at Yale University found evidence of hemoglobin and other blood pigments, and an Italian forensic medicine professor named Pierluigi Baima-Bollone identified type AB human blood. Furthermore blood samples from the Shroud were analyzed in Texas University Health Science Center, where they found evidence of human DNA and the male XY chromosome. In other words, the stains are not painted on—a male human body was wrapped by this cloth.[10]

Naturally, some people still believe that the Shroud is just an artistic representation of Jesus' dead body. The author of this masterpiece remains anonymous; no one has claimed the credit or glory for creating such a brilliant "forgery." Moreover, no one has been able to determine the technique used.

WHAT DOES THE EVIDENCE PROVE?

At the beginning of this section I stated that an integral part of my approach to complex issues is simplicity. My simple logic leaves me with many questions:

1. What is the rationale of going through such a complex set of research techniques—just to keep people guessing?
2. Artists like to claim their work, especially, masterpieces. Why has no one claimed it?
3. If the Shroud is a fraud that employs medieval painting techniques, it is very unlikely that all of our modern, twenty-first-century scientific tools cannot explain how it was done. The rationale behind any fraud is that "it can be reproduced." So why can't we make it happen again?

For some reason, the more we study it, the more confusing it gets.

It is not my intention to make a case for the Shroud; I just want to simplify a complex scientific dilemma. I will leave you with what I believe is the safest position—the STURP conclusion:

We can conclude for now that the Shroud image is that of a real human form of a scourged, crucified man. It is not the product of an artist. The blood stains are composed of hemoglobin and also give a positive test for serum albumin. The image is an ongoing mystery and until further chemical studies are made, perhaps by this group of scientists, or perhaps by some scientists in the future, the problem remains unsolved.[11]

Chapter 2

HISTORICAL BACKGROUND

Monarchs, empires, and civilizations come and go, but religions seems to go for ever.[1]

S
ince ancient times, there has been a need to conquer and control the fate of other countries. Great empires dominated weaker nations by utilizing overwhelming military force. The propensity for violence is very well established in the history of humanity.

At the beginning of the Imperial era the Greeks used to make their colonies accept and practice the religion and traditions of the Empire. This practice required submission by violent intimidation. As the Imperial era progressed, religions and some traditions of the native colonies were preserved. By the time Israel was incorporated into the Roman Empire, the colonies were allowed to preserve certain of their own traits, examples of which are religious traditions and some political power.

The successions of emperors also brought different styles to the handling of the colonies because of individual differences among the emperors. In other words, some emperors were more tolerant than others. Yet it is safe to say that overwhelming force and brutality were key components of the strategy to keep the colonies under control.

It was customary in ancient civilizations to publicly execute criminals in a barbaric way as a means of intimidating and controlling criminal behavior. There have been several methods of execution through the history of mankind. Some of the methods were initially a form of torture to obtain information, but the brutality was such that the victim did not survive. Infamous methods of torture and execution included the spiked collar, the witch's chair, the coffin, the rack, the iron maiden, and the brazen bull. The brazen bull, a method of torture invented by the Greeks, was exceptionally brutal. The victim was placed inside the hollow statue of a bull made out of metal, and fire was ignited underneath until it became red-hot, cooking the victim to death. It was designed in such a way that the screams from the victim projected as music coming from the bull's mouth.

But no other form of execution in the history of humanity could match the degree of brutality of crucifixion—lashing and nailing a victim to a wooden beam until he died.

CRUCIFIXION

The actual inventor of this brutal method of capital punishment has not been established, but it is well known that the Persians utilized it when they conquered Egypt and Carthage (539–526 BC). Subsequently, The Greeks, led by Alexander the Great, took over the Persian colonies. As the Greek colonies became Roman colonies in the period from 149–146 BC, the Romans were exposed to crucifixion. Having become familiar with this method of execution in Carthage, they then perfected it.

HISTORICAL KEY EVENTS[2]

• Israelites in Egypt	400 years
• Moses leads Israel to the Promised Land	1250 BC
• King David	1000 to 961 BC
• King Solomon builds temple, Jerusalem	950 BC
• Jews deported	597 to 586 BC
• Persians conquer Babylon and Egypt	539 and 526 BC
• Alexander the Great conquers Egypt	332 BC
• Alexander the Great conquers Persia	328 BC
• Rome conquers Carthage	149 to 146 BC
• Romans conquer the Holy Land	63 BC
• Jesus born in Bethlehem	1-6 BC
• Jesus crucified, resurrected	AD 30

Crucifixion became the standard method of intimidation and punishment against the enemies and potential threats of the Roman Empire. It is important to note that crucifixion was not employed against Roman citizens unless they were accused of treason. In other words, it was reserved for foreigners and the oppressed citizens of the colony.

The execution took place in strategic areas outside the city limits, always in highly visible locations. The idea was to have the victim exposed to the view of passersby coming in and out of the city. It is important to understand that this method of execution was designed to cause extreme pain and suffering over a long period of time. You would expect that, as a rule of thumb, the more painful the punishment, the faster the victim should die. Well, this rule does not apply to crucifixion as a method of execution.

As people would come upon the crucifixion site, it would not be unusual to see several crucified victims at different stages of the process. Just imagine this scene: multiple bodies hanging on different poles, some of them already dead for days, others gasping and fighting for their next breath. Obviously, the scene would be overwhelmingly frightening and intimidating, which of course was the goal.

Through the crucifixion of Jesus, the Roman Empire gave this instrument of brutal torture the spotlight in history. The cross became the symbol of the followers of Jesus.

In health care, the word "excruciating" is used to describe unbearable and overwhelming pain, for example, excruciating pain in the abdomen. This particular word sets off an alarm in a physician's mind; a potentially lethal condition might be developing in the patient's abdomen. *Excruciate* is a Latin compound word that means "out of the cross."

In our society, the cross has also become a symbol that represents other painful situations. You have probably heard expressions like "to carry this cross" referring to an emotional or physical burden or "I will crucify you," which is an obvious, serious threat. The bottom line is that "cross" is never neutral; it equates with severe, unbearable pain on every level, even death. Keep this fact in mind as we explore the extreme physical and mental burden that Jesus suffered when he was crucified.

The Hebrews Under Roman Domination

In the year 63 BC, the whole region of Palestine and its primary city, Jerusalem, became a Roman colony. Later, in the year 40 BC, the Roman senate designated Herod the Great as the king of the Jews. He became very well known as a tyrant. We need to remember that he was the one, after the time of Jesus' birth, who authorized the assassination of all of the children two years old and under, with the goal of eliminating the potential Messiah.

After the death of Herod the Great, the kingdom was divided among his three sons: Archelaus, Herod Antipas, and Philip. Archelaus was assigned to rule Judea and Samaria. It appears as though Archelaus inherited the cruelty of his father. He was such a cruel ruler that even the Roman Empire could not tolerate him. He was removed from office and Pontius Pilate, a Roman prefect, was assigned to govern Judea and Samaria, directly answerable to the Roman emperor, who had the ultimate power and the last word.

Tax collections were all-important for the Empire. Indeed, 35 percent of any income or business transaction went to pay the empire tax. This financial setup became an enormous burden for the colony and created a huge gap between upper class and lower class.[3]

A very powerful religious class came into prominence, one with extraordinary social and political influence: the Sanhedrin and the priests. This religious-social class enjoyed special consideration from the Roman Empire. It is safe to say that the Sanhedrin and the priests constituted an aristocratic group that was disconnected from the social realities of the lower class.

As a result, Jewish society was divided in two. The rich, powerful aristocrats and religious leaders were on one side and the uneducated, poor, and pagans on the other. Discrimination was the norm. Women were considered inferior. According to the Jewish historian, Flavius Josephus, "The woman, in all aspects, is of less value than the man."[4] Children and pagans also belonged to the lower class. The Samaritans, the people from the northern part of Israel, were for all practical purposes ignored.

The lower class was hoping for a revolutionary leader to change this unfair reality. At the same time, the upper class wanted a military leader to get rid of Rome and reestablish their independent Jewish dynasty (hopefully while allowing them to keep their current privileges). Freedom from Rome's tyranny meant different things to the two different classes, but everyone wanted to be delivered from the conquering power.

This was the fragmented and discontented society into which Jesus was born.

CHAPTER 3

JESUS CHRIST—
THE MESSIAH

But you, Bethlehem Ephrathah, though you are small among the clans of Judah, out of you will come for me one who will be ruler over Israel, whose origins are from of old, from ancient times.

Therefore Israel will be abandoned until the time when she who is in labor bears a son, and the rest of his brothers return to join the Israelites.

MICAH 5:2–3

The Old Testament reveals the unique relationship between God and the nation of Israel. Throughout the history of Israel, the commitment of God to his people is evident. His unlimited patience is tested again and again. Each time his beloved nation has walked away from the covenant, he has found ways to guide them back to greatness. Sometimes the path was preceded by extreme duress in the form of slavery and exile. In those moments of extreme anxiety, poverty, and sadness, Israel would put its fate back into the hands of God. Those moments of full devotion to the Lord were always answered or followed by the reestablishment of great things for the nation. Whenever Israel followed God's will, they enjoyed happiness, strength, and contentment. Then, after the passage of a certain amount of time, Israel would shift away from God again. But in his unlimited patience, God carried them along.

Over the centuries, God gave a very special gift to a select group of individuals: the gift of carrying his divine message to his people, Israel.

These individuals were the prophets. It appears as though the prophets' messages could be divided into three types: warnings about current behavior, punishments if the behavior did not cease, and, last but not least, prophecies of hope.

The warning messages were given to God's people for years, even for generations, before a punishment. Their Assyrian captivity, for example, was predicted seven hundred years prior to when it occurred. The prophets were unrelenting as they reminded the people of what could happen to them as a consequence of their sins.

Then, during a time of captivity, the prophets would announce their upcoming greatness if the nation would only start following its covenant with God again. I believe that just as the misery and difficulties in the nation of Israel were brought about by the sin of the people and just as their reformed lives could return them to peace and joy, so we too can reach out to God in our difficulties and find him again. But we tend to neglect the worship of God when we are enjoying security and prosperity.

THE COMING MESSIAH

For Israel, always the prophets promised a coming leader who would be so great that he would fight for them and get them out of captivity and out of misery for good. Thus for a long time, the Jews had been waiting for a powerful leader with unprecedented power, someone who would be capable of guiding them to freedom and greatness—a messiah.

Somewhere in their history, however, their expectations about what this messiah should be like got twisted. He started to be defined in terms of characteristics such as military might and social power. After all, the legendary men in their history, such as Moses or King David, had guided them to freedom and greatness.

The prophet Micah announced the Messiah somewhere around 722 BC. He was very specific about the Messiah's place of birth: Bethlehem. This small, simple village, home of the Davidic line, is now known in the history of Israel and in the history of the whole world as the birthplace of the Messiah. Greatness comes from simplicity.

Here are the words of the prophet Isaiah about the Messiah:

> Every warrior's boot used in battle and every garment rolled in blood
> will be destined for burning, will be fuel for the fire.
> For to us a child is born, to us a son is given, and the government
> will be on his shoulders.
> And he will be called Wonderful Counselor, Mighty God, Everlasting
> Father, Prince of Peace.
> Of the greatness of his government and peace there will be no end.
> He will reign on David's throne and over his kingdom, establishing
> and upholding it with justice and righteousness from that time
> on and forever.
> The zeal of the Lord Almighty will accomplish this. (Isaiah 9:5–7)

The prophet Isaiah gives us more information regarding the characteristics of this Messiah. In this prophecy, we find a very strong statement against violence: "…every garment rolled in blood will be destined for burning, will be fuel for the fire." It also shows us three important backbones of the kingdom of God: peace, justice, and righteousness. These three elements will support the Messiah's forever-lasting kingdom.

I am always amazed when I see how the ancient prophecies came to life in the New Testament—including the birth of Jesus in Bethlehem, his ministry, his teaching, his method of death, and even his resurrection. His three-year ministry was filled with deeds of compassion and preaching about peace, justice, and righteousness.

As student, I always liked to use analogies to help me remember important information. There is no doubt that the whole Trinity concept is overwhelming, even for the most seasoned theologian. The coexistence of three divine beings in one God is way beyond my comprehension. But I know that the day I feel I can understand everything about God, he will no longer be God.

Even though I realize that I can never understand everything about

God, I have a lot of curiosity about him. I want to investigate everything about him, and I enjoy the process. Sometimes my daily experiences give me new insights. Here's an example of something that happened during a surgery. The surgical suite is a unique environment where an interesting mixture of personalities joins in the effort to take care of a patient. During an operation, a key constituent is the anesthesiologist, who makes sure that the patient doesn't feel any pain while the surgery is performed. I have found that one of the cardiac anesthesiologist at my institution has the ability to really simplify concepts. Once during an open-heart procedure, we were having a conversation about religion right there in the surgical suite. One of the members of the team was very confused about Jesus. This particular cardiac anesthesiologists supplied us with the simplest definition about Jesus I had ever heard: "He is a photocopy of God, faxed to Earth."

I wanted to share this with my readers, because I was so thrilled with this clever definition. What a great and practical way to describe Jesus and his relationship with the Father!

And this Jesus is the Messiah, the Savior, the one sent by the Father to bring anyone who will follow him back to God:

> Let us run with perseverance the race marked out for us, fixing our eyes on Jesus, the pioneer and perfecter of faith. For the joy set before him he endured the cross, scorning its shame, and sat down at the right hand of the throne of God.

Hebrews 12:1–2

Jesus, the Man

You might not realize this, but when you visit a doctor, the physical exam begins long before he or she places the stethoscope on your chest. It starts before there is any physical contact. It might start with the greetings and how you answer the greetings. It is called observation. There is an interview where you answer questions about your family medical history, previous medical issues, or surgical problems that you might have had in the past. This interview should go all the way back to prenatal care and childhood. The process of the medical interview plus the physical exam generates a document called clinical history, but it is most commonly called history and physical (H&P). The long curriculum of medical school includes assignments that allow physicians to use their senses at the time of examining a patient.

In my examination of Jesus, the man, I have applied my medical and surgical training to evaluating his health prior to his crucifixion. There are a couple of sources that can provide relevant information regarding his physical and psychological shape prior to his arrest and crucifixion.

We can start with the prenatal period. There is no evidence in the history as presented in the Bible that Mary had any potential hereditary condition that could be inherited by Jesus. It appears that she was in good health (both physical and psychological) prior to the pregnancy. The angel who told her she was going to become the mother of the Messiah simply told her that she was the chosen one for this unprecedented role:

> The angel said to her, "Do not be afraid, Mary; you have found favor with God. You will conceive and give birth to a son, and you are to call him Jesus. He will be great and will be called the Son of the Most High. The Lord God will give him the throne of his father David."
>
> LUKE 1:30–32

Mary became pregnant by the grace of the Holy Spirit. She had no health issues during her pregnancy. In other words, the prenatal period appears to have been normal. In nine months, she gave birth to baby Jesus in Bethlehem.

THE STAR OF BETHLEHEM AND DATE OF JESUS' BIRTH

After Jesus was born in Bethlehem in Judea, during the time of King Herod, Magi from the east came to Jerusalem and asked,

"Where is the one who has been born king of the Jews? We saw his star when it rose and have come to worship him."

MATTHEW 2:1–2

Christmas is such a special time of the year. Families put effort into getting the house ready for the season. One of the most spectacular decorations is the bright star on top of the Christmas tree. Some people believe that the "star of Bethlehem" is only a symbol to give more brightness to the occasion. They forget that, historically, royal births and other events have always been associated with special stars. Of course, most traditional Christians just accept that God decided to put a huge star in the sky of Bethlehem when Jesus was born, simply because he is God and he can do that if he wants to.

Not long ago, I had the joy of watching the documentary *The Star of Bethlehem* by Frederick Larson. It is a masterpiece. The producer has been able to explain the mystery of the star of Bethlehem with very sound astronomical information. Larson stimulated my interest in this feature of Jesus' birth as an historical astronomical event. I have to acknowledge that I had no idea that astronomy is such a reliable and accurate science, based on mathematical calculations that are so precise that they are not only capable of predicting the position of the planets and stars in the future, but equally capable of looking at astronomical activity at any particular moment in the history of humanity.

The search for the star mentioned in Matthew is nothing new. Johannes Kepler (1571–1630), one of the greatest mathematicians of all times, figured out that planets travel in elliptical orbits and he was then able to predict the planetary movements. Kepler established the laws of the planetary motion that are used today by modern astronomers and space agencies such as NASA. This great scientist was also a Christian, and he tried to find the star of Matthew. Unfortunately, he was not able to find the star because he looked in the wrong time frame. Misled by the wrong dates provided by copy errors of Flavius Josephus' historical manuscripts, he used the year 6 BC instead of the year 2 or 3 BC as has been done more recently.

Needless to say, historically people have used a lot of paper and ink in order to manually calculate the sky map for any given time. Nowadays, computer software can do these calculations very easily. Modern software can produce both a map of the sky on a particular date (past, present, or future) and a picture of the sky on that date, as it would look from a specific location.

Using the "Starry Night" software, we can look at the sky over Bethlehem between the years 3 and 2 BC. Let us see what the Magi were going after.

The star of Bethlehem was the conjunction between Jupiter and the star Regulus. This is a map of the sky of Bethlehem in September, 3 BC, as shown by the astronomy software Starry Night.

So the star described by Matthew is real after all; the mysterious star is the planet Jupiter as viewed in conjunction with the star Regulus. Apparently, a very dynamic conjunction occurred between these two, and it caught the attention of those ancient astronomers called the Magi. In other words, the story described by Matthew has very sound astronomical explanation. God used his own creation to write the most important story of the world in the sky.

It is difficult to ascertain the date of Jesus' birth. As mentioned earlier, copy errors in Josephus' manuscript placed Herod's death in 4 BC. According to the biblical account, Jesus was born during Herod's reign. And it can be inferred that Jesus was born about two years prior to Herod's death, which would seem to be around 6 BC. Recent research, however, discovered the copy errors; now it appears that Herod's death occurred in the year 1 BC. Based on this revised date, we can indirectly assume that Jesus was born somewhere between 3 and 2 BC. In the two-year period between 3 and 1 BC, several historical/biblical events took place—the visit of the Magi following the star of Bethlehem and also the horrific assassination of the innocent males babies under two years of age that was ordered by Herod. These indirect evidences are nevertheless logical, and the astronomical calculations seem to prove them.[1]

In order to illustrate the complexity of this subject, I have included two tables compiled by different authors; each provides a distinct timetable regarding Jesus' birthday.

COLIN HUMPHREYS'S CHRONOLOGY OF THE NATIVITY[2]

Date	Event
5 BC	
March 9 – May 4	Birth of Jesus in Bethlehem
March 9 – May 4	Visit of the shepherds
March 16 – May 11	Circumcision
April 18 – June 13	Presentation at the temple in Jerusalem and return to Bethlehem
April 20 – June 15	Visit of the Magi
Late April – Mid-June	Flight to Egypt
4 BC	
Late March	Death of Herod

DAVID HUGHES'S PUBLISHED CHRONOLOGY OF THE NATIVITY[3]

9 – 6 BC	Saturnius, governor of Syria
	Quirinius, emperor's legate
8 BC	Augustus Caesar decrees that all should be taxed
7 – 5 BC	Biblical date of the birth of Jesus
6 – 5 BC	Slaughter of the innocents
4 BC	
March 13	Eclipse of the Moon
March 13 – April 11	Death of Herod
April 11	Start of Passover
3 BC	
November 18	Nativity according to Clement
2 BC	
January 6	Nativity according to Epiphanius
AD 1	
December 25	Nativity according to Dionysius Exiguus

JESUS' CHILDHOOD

There is not too much information about Jesus' childhood. It is documented that part of his childhood was in Egypt, where his parents took him for safety's sake. (The angel of God instructed Joseph to take the boy to Egypt to avoid any potential danger from King Herod, who had ordered the execution of every male child under the age of two, hoping to eliminate the young Messiah.)

Once the danger was over, the family returned to the town of Nazareth in Galilee, where they lived for Jesus' remaining childhood years. Luke gives a short but specific summary of Jesus' childhood:

> When Joseph and Mary had done everything required by the Law of the Lord, they returned to Galilee, to their own town of Nazareth. And the child grew and became strong: he was filled with wisdom; and the grace of God was on him.

LUKE 2:39–40

When Jesus reached the age of twelve, he and his parents travelled to Jerusalem as was customary, for the Passover feast. After the feast, Jesus stayed in Jerusalem without his parents noticing. Once they realized it (after three days), they returned to Jerusalem, where they found him at the temple, in the midst of a very dynamic conversation about the Scripture. His high level of knowledge at that young age proved to be very puzzling to the scholars with whom he was speaking. Imagine it: a twelve-year-old staying behind when his parents left with their group. He was alone, by himself in the big city of Jerusalem. Was this like a "teenager moment"? When his heavyhearted parents finally located him, where was he? Off having some teenage fun with others his own age? No, he was not found playing with other teens; he was conversing with learned men of God at the house of his heavenly Father, the temple.

This episode of the boy Jesus in the temple is the most complete documented scene concerning Jesus' post-infancy childhood. The Gospel-writer Luke's assessment of Jesus' childhood is a historical testimony that Jesus grew up as a normal child. It appears that throughout his remaining adolescent years as well as through his twenties, he stayed "under the radar," keeping a low profile and living the ordinary life of a carpenter's son, helping his father, Joseph with his work.

The sparse biblical account has stimulated a significant amount of speculation regarding the "missing" years. People have said that he must have traveled to different parts of the world and became familiar with other cultural, philosophical, and religious traditions. Some have assumed that during that period he somehow became familiar with yoga and other forms of mind and body control. Others have hypothesized that he became an extraordinary illusionist because he traveled to India, where he learned all kind of tricks.

I agree that Jesus performed all kind of amazing feats, but random speculation is not a good way to explain what we cannot understand. The bottom line is that no documentation exists of any journey to exotic and mysterious places during those years. It is safe to assume only that during those years he grew up strong physically and mentally, as stated by Luke. As was customary in his country, he learned his father's trade, becoming a carpenter like his human father, Joseph. (Most likely in those days a "carpenter" was more like what we call a handyman. This assumption is based on the type of simple constructions used in that era and in that region.)

I do have my own curiosity regarding Jesus' adolescent years. My biggest question is this: When did he realize that he was the Son of God? By looking at the episode of the young Jesus in the temple, I think it is safe to say that he already knew at least by age twelve. Let's look again at that episode and read between the lines a little:

> When his parents saw him, they were astonished. His mother said to him, "Son, why have you treated us like this? Your father and I have been anxiously searching for you."
>
> "Why were you searching for me?" he asked. "Didn't you know I had to be in my Father's house?" But they did not understand what he was saying to them.
>
> Then he went down to Nazareth with them and was obedient to them. But his mother treasured all these things in her heart. And Jesus grew in wisdom and stature, and in favor with God and man.
>
> LUKE 2:48–52

We can see from the answer he gave to his parents that it was kind of a friendly reminder to them about his divine nature. The Christian faith teaches us that Jesus is God and that he shares our human nature. My physician's mind can't stop thinking about God sharing our human nature. At some point, that God was sharing the human nature of an adolescent child. That is scary, isn't it? Dealing with an adolescent child can be challenging, as anyone who has parented an adolescent understands. I am curious about how Jesus was perceived by his playmates: Was he a model boy and a good example for the others, or was he indistinguishable from them? Was there at some point any turmoil between the divine nature and that teenage nature? How did he deal with that? Remember that adolescence implies some degree of rebellion, which is part of that stage of human development. He was human as well as God.

I think it's safe to assume that he had a normal adolescence, whatever that meant in first-century Nazareth, although I am not sure that the concept of "normal" can be applied here.

Then at age thirty, Jesus emerged as a young enigmatic and charismatic leader whose presence created an enormous upheaval in Jewish society and later on the Roman Empire.

Jesus: Language and Literacy

I have found that researching Jesus is a very dynamic enterprise, because there are so many different points of view regarding all aspects of his life. Even a trivial issue such as what language or languages he spoke has been subject of debate. And it does get more complicated when researching whether or not he could read and write. As I mentioned earlier, I consider a pre-crucifixion medical profile to be an intrinsic component of this project. Part of the clinical evaluation includes the level of education as well as what the patient (victim, in this case) did for a living. I thought that finding out what language or languages he spoke, his level of education, and whether or not he could read would be an easy task. But the scholars have not made it easy at all.

To simplify this topic, I needed to settle the historical and social facts regarding Jesus' time. As has been historically established, Judea was a Roman colony in the time of Jesus. During the first century and in that particular region, Aramaic was the predominant language.[4] The region appears to have been a cultural melting pot. We know, for instance, that Hebrew and Greek were also widely spoken.[5] (Remember that the Greek colonies became Roman colonies.) It is useful to look at the Greek as the equivalent of English nowadays. In other words, Greek was the *lingua franca*—the language used in diplomacy, business, and scientific meetings where the participants belonged to countries with different idioms.

Clear evidence in the Bible indicates that Aramaic was Jesus' primary language. But we do have to keep an open mind to the possibility of Jesus being multilingual. The rationale for that possibility is based on the cultural melting pot mentioned earlier. The young Jews were growing up with enough exposure to three languages to allow them to master them. It is also important to understand that the Aramaic and the Hebrew are relatively closely related. A comparison to Spanish and Portuguese can help us to understand the relationship between languages.

(In fact, I didn't realize how similar Spanish and Portuguese were until I came to the United States in 1990, and I was asked to help a Brazilian patient with some translation in the hospital. Initially, I was not enthusiastic about it because I thought the two different languages are too dissimilar. It was a pleasant surprise to find out that we were able to communicate very well. I had never been exposed to Portuguese. Now, imagine how much better I would have done if I had had a regular exposure to it!)

The whole thing about the languages becomes somewhat more complex when we try to figure out where Latin fits into these possibilities. For a long time, I have wondered what language must have been used in the most important trial of human history. Jesus was facing the Roman prefect, Pilate. If he used Latin, then either Jesus spoke some Latin, or they had a translator who hasn't been mentioned anywhere. It is my belief that Greek, the primary or trade language, must have been used in this historical trial. I might be wrong in my assumption, but it does not seem likely that Hebrew or Aramaic was the language used in that particular trial.

Then, in terms of literacy, could Jesus read or write? This particular question has been also the subject of substantial debate; the scholars are all over the place on this one. The opinions vary from an absolute "no" to an absolute "yes." I should add that somehow the range between the "no" and the "yes" is also wide.

I have to believe that the answer to that question can be found by understanding some of the social, cultural, and religious traditions of Judea. As very well stated by James D. G. Dunn in his book, *Jesus Remembered*, traditional Judaism placed enormous emphasis on the study of the Torah.[6] In other words, the Jewish religious establishment stimulated this particular Roman colony to learn to read. In the historical context where he grew up, and based on the socio-cultural and religious environment of the time, it is quite possible that Jesus was literate.[7] To help settle the forever-lasting debate about this particular subject, why not simply trust the very words of the Bible?—

> He went to Nazareth, where he had been brought up, and on the Sabbath day he went into the synagogue, as was his custom. *He stood up to read.* The scroll of the prophet Isaiah was handed to him. Unrolling it, he found the place where it is written:
> "The Spirit of the Lord is on me,
> because he has anointed me
> to preach good news to the poor.
> He has sent me to proclaim freedom for the prisoners
> and recovery of sight for the blind,
> to release the oppressed,
> to proclaim the year of the Lord's favor."
> Then he rolled up the scroll, gave it back to the attendant and sat down. The eyes of everyone in the synagogue were fastened on him, and he began by saying to them, "Today this scripture is fulfilled in your hearing."
>
> LUKE 4:16–21, EMPHASIS ADDED

It is very clear in this passage that he could read. In fact, it is loud and clear. But some investigators can make any subject a very complex one. Some people make a living out of controversies. Again, let's keep it simple; Jews, traditionally, aim for high standards in education, and this is not new. This tradition of high standards in education is well documented by the Jewish historian Josephus in his book, *Against Apion*, in which he describes the Jewish commitment to education:

> Our principal care of all is this, to educate our children well; and we think it to be the most necessary business of our whole life to observe the laws that have been given us, and to keep

those rules of piety that have been delivered down to us.[8]
...It also commands us to bring those children up in learning, and to exercise them in the laws, and make them acquainted
with the acts of their predecessors.[9]

It seems obvious to me that we don't need to know what public
school Jesus went to in order to agree that he could read. Also, as very
well described by Dunn, the educational emphasis of Judaism probably
lowered the illiteracy rate of the Hebrews compared to that of other
Roman colonies. I do believe that, based on the time and culture in which
he lived, Jesus was most likely multi-linguistic and literate.

JESUS' MINISTRY

We live in a technological era. News travels fast; in fact, we are bom-
barded continuously with news everywhere. We can't hide from the
media. The Web and satellite TV have closed the distance between countries, creating a virtual nation. Any public figure or leader has the ability
to reach the public in many different ways, and they also know how to
achieve virtual interaction with their followers. Nowadays, it is unthink-
able that a prestigious leader would not use modern communication
tools to reach out to the public.

Now, imagine a time long ago, without even telephones. Think about
how difficult it must have been to send communications to other places.
Think about how hard it must have been to become a public figure.
Long-distance transportation required animals such as camels and
horses. How difficult it was to transmit a message and reach a significant
amount of people.

Jesus started his ministry when he was around thirty years old, but
his activities were not covered in the evening news. It appears the starting
point occurred at a wedding in the small town of Cana, where he performed his first documented miracle (see John 2:1–11). At the wedding,
he transformed jugs of water into wine when the host ran out of wine. I
find it interesting that he took care of something like that. This episode

tells me how much he cared about his friends. (Let's not underestimate the importance of wine in a wedding. It was as important then as it is now. If you have ever organized a wedding, you know exactly what I mean.) After this wedding, one thing led to another and suddenly he found himself in the midst of his ministry. He went from being the son of Joseph, the carpenter, to an amazing public figure.

The social fabric of Israel was seriously frayed. As I mentioned earlier, discrimination was the rule. Somehow, the political-religious leaders managed to find support in the Scriptures for their unfair, discriminatory establishment. The whole idea that all men were equals in the eyes of God had been buried long before. The grace of God was supposed to belong to or favor only one social group: rich and educated men.

Jesus' preaching was 180 degrees opposite to the traditional preaching. In his three-year ministry, he focused on demonstrating that because God created humans in his image, we are all his children, and that the rule of discrimination was not acceptable. It was obvious from the start that Jesus' position against the established regime placed him on a collision course with the authorities, who were offended and threatened by him.

Somehow, even without a means of mass communication, Jesus managed to reach vast numbers of people. Can we analyze some of the strategies that he used to increase his reach to the population? One key strategy was the recruitment of disciples, a method that was used commonly in ancient times. Disciples would abandon their jobs and families to follow a master. They received a 24/7 training, and following their leader became a lifestyle.

Jesus chose twelve ordinary men to follow him. It was like a mobile monastery. Their daily life combined teaching, meditation, and observation of Jesus interacting with people who were not his disciples. Jesus' inner group included a wide variety of men from different backgrounds, ranging from fishermen to a tax collector. The Master made sure that a cross-section of society was represented in his inner circle. As we know well even today, tax collectors were not very popular, and yet Matthew left his tax-collecting duties to follow Jesus. I believe that by including such a variety of people, he sent an important message: "God wants to include everybody in his kingdom."

This intense teaching method allowed Jesus, in a short period of time, to educate and transfer as much information to his disciples as possible. Afterwards, the disciples were able to go to many different places, sharing the Good News wherever they went. This was a very effective way for Jesus to increase his reach.

Jesus' public dissertations in strategic places provided him with more public exposure. When he spoke, Jesus taught crowds of people about the real meaning of the sacred Scriptures. The whole spectrum of topics was explained in very simple language, understandable to every citizen regardless of educational level. There was something different about this young rabbi; he was explaining the Scriptures with a very unique authority and teaching about the real meaning of life. It was almost as if he was the author!

Jesus took advantage of small crowds, too. Once a crowd had come together, other bystanders would be attracted to investigate what was happening. Curiosity brought more and more people to hear him. In the meantime, this new leader was also matching his actions with his words; he was living and leading by example.

All of this gives us some idea about the impact of Jesus among his followers. But still one of Jesus' most incredible powers hasn't been addressed: miracles. I suppose that miracles might have different meanings for different people. But here we are not talking about an extraordinary event that can be explained by careful analysis of natural laws. We are talking about events that cannot be explained, even by a rigorous analysis of the natural laws. Jesus performed plenty of miracles that defied rational explanation. Not only did he transform plain water into wedding-quality wine and multiply a few small loaves of bread to feed an enormous crowd, he also walked on water, healed all kind of illness—and raised the dead.

He always attached a miracle to a particular message. For example, "I am the bread of life" was tied to the multiplication of the bread. He did not perform miracles just to answer a challenge from an infidel; faith was an integral part of the miracle scene. It is easy to imagine the huge impact in a town when a well-known blind person is now capable of seeing again, or a mute is suddenly praising the Lord.

As I analyzed his ministry, I asked myself what would have happened if he had not done any miracles? What kind of impact would he have had in his society? What impact would he have had on us, citizens of this century?

Regardless of miracles, of one thing I am sure: he already had earned a unique position in history as a religious, moral leader. The miracles launched him up to a different level—a level that only he belongs to—his own category. In a short three-year ministry, Jesus' name became well-known in spite of the transportation limitations and the lack of Internet or TV. Judea was on fire!

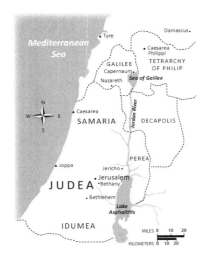

Territory covered by Jesus
in his ministry

PERSONALITY OF JESUS

Most of the definitions of personality refer to the qualities that make a human being uniquely him- or herself. *The Stedman's Medical Dictionary* defines personality as the "totality of qualities and traits, as of character or behavior, that are peculiar to a specific person."[10]

Naturally, it is somewhat complex to describe the personality of an historical figure accurately, because the analysis must be based on the interpretation of written documents. In real life, person-to-person interaction is the key to the valid perception of personalities, and some personality traits will be perceived differently by different individuals. With Jesus, all we have to go on are the written stories about his life on Earth. I have found it very interesting to seek to discover more about his personality by analyzing certain episodes of his life. In fact, some episodes turn out to be extremely educational from a psychological standpoint.

The best place to learn about Jesus' personality is the Bible, more specifically, the Gospels. For instance, in Matthew 6, some of Jesus' traits and personality are shown through his recommendations about how to pray:

> But when you pray, go into your room, close the door and pray to your Father, who is unseen. Then your Father, who sees what is done in secret, will reward you. And when you pray, do not keep on babbling like pagans, for they think they will be heard because of their many words. (Matthew 6:6–7)

Jesus recommends praying in secret in a quiet place and not using too many words. This particular recommendation reveals a person who appreciates quiet times as well as private interactions with the Father. It also reflects his preference for using language efficiently. He sees no reason to use a hundred words if you can say the same thing with twenty-five. It looks to me that we are in the presence of a simple, private, and straightforward man. Although Jesus' commitment to his mission made him a public figure, it is obvious that, even with his status, privacy was highly important to him. We find multiple passages in the Bible that tell about times when he removed himself to pray and meditate in silence, by himself.

I find Jesus to be very consistent regarding simplicity in wording. Based on Jesus' way of praying as documented in the Bible, it is easy to conclude that we do not need to use clever wording when we talk to our Father. In fact, if you review Jesus' speeches, including the Sermon on the Mount in Matthew 5, there is no complex wording whatsoever. His message is simple enough for everybody to understand. His simple style should be an example for some leaders today, when they try to impress the public with a very sophisticated vocabulary.

Simplicity is not only a key element of his prayers and teachings, but simplicity in the wording can also be seen in God's mystical appearances in the Old Testament. Look at God's interaction with Moses and notice the simplicity of his vocabulary:

"Do not come any closer," God said. "Take off your sandals, for the place where you are standing is holy ground." Then he said, "I am the God of your father, the God of Abraham, the God of Isaac and the God of Jacob." At this, Moses hid his face, because he was afraid to look at God. (Exodus 3:5–6)

It appears that simple wording is a common denominator between both the Father and the Son. We ourselves certainly do not need to impress God with sophisticated wording or too many words. After all, he knows what we are about to say before we utter a word.

Another episode in the Bible that reflects not only Jesus' personality but also his own knowledge of human psychology is the story about the woman who had been caught in adultery. I will include the whole story in order to fully appreciate Jesus' demonstration of self-control in the face of an obvious trap:

The teachers of the law and the Pharisees brought in a woman caught in adultery. They made her stand before the group and said to Jesus, "Teacher, this woman was caught in the act of adultery. In the Law Moses commanded us to stone such women. Now what do you say?" They were using this question as a trap, in order to have a basis for accusing him.

But Jesus bent down and started to write on the ground with his finger. When they kept on questioning him, he straightened up and said to them, "Let any one of you who is without sin be the first to throw a stone at her." Again he stooped down and wrote on the ground.

At this, those who heard began to go away one at a time, the older ones first, until only Jesus was left, with the woman still standing there. Jesus straightened up and asked her,

"Woman, where are they? Has no one condemned you?"

"No one, sir," she said.

"Then neither do I condemn you," Jesus declared. "Go now and leave your life of sin."

JOHN 8:3–11

Imagine a very calm, tall male surrounded by a group of aggressive individuals. They set up a trap for him by asking a specific question regarding adultery. Jesus took his time, bending down and starting to write something in the dirt. Maybe he was just doing that to take his time, to come up with a strategy, to choose the appropriate words. Then the enigmatic Jesus slowly stood up and delivered a classic neutralizing statement, "Let any one of you who is without sin be the first to throw a stone at her."

In this episode, he demonstrated supreme self-control. It could have turned ugly. The mob seemed to be ready to stone the woman and it wouldn't have taken much to send them out of control. Jesus had perfect control of the whole scene and a thorough understanding of mob psychology.

Stoning a woman caught committing adultery was justifiable under the Law of Moses, and the men might have had short fuses because they were perpetually frustrated with their powerlessness under Roman rule. Jesus' calm approach to this scene was paramount in avoiding escalation in the aggressiveness of the crowd. It is a well-known principle in human behavior that aggressiveness generates more aggressiveness. Jesus' key psychological strategy was to avoid too much body language and to remain calm. A lack of control on his part would have cost the life of the woman, himself, and his disciples.

PHYSICAL ASPECTS OF THE MAN OF THE SHROUD

Although the authenticity of the Shroud of Turin remains controversial, for the purpose of this section, I would like to assume its authenticity in order to describe some of the likely physical characteristics of the victim.

The human whose figure appears on the shroud was a male with type AB blood. He stood between 5'9 to 5'11" and weighed approximately 170 pounds. In health care, a calculation called the Body Mass Index, or BMI, provides a reliable indicator of body fat. This calculation is used to screen for weight-related health problems. Jesus' BMI shows he was a normal weight, not overweight or obese by any means, with a well-proportioned body that could even be considered athletic. It is also important to realize that a 5'11" Jewish male was fairly tall for that era.

Prior to his crucifixion, Jesus was a 33-year-old in very good physical shape, to judge by his height/weight ratio and more. Surely his background as a carpenter required a significant amount of physical endurance. During his three-year ministry, he and his disciples covered an extraordinary amount of territory on foot. (See Fig. 5, map of territory covered by Jesus in his ministry.)

If you take everything together—his perfect physique, his communication skills, his authoritative statements, and his commitment to the poorest people—anyone can see why the authorities became threatened by this young man. With extraordinary magnetism and charisma, Jesus projected himself as a rightful leader, knowledgeable and caring toward the people who followed him willingly. Doubtless the authorities were intimidated by his ability to connect with and influence the people. As his leadership continued to grow exponentially, he was becoming too popular. He had to be eliminated.

CHAPTER 4

THE CRUCIFIXION

While they were eating, Jesus took bread, and when he had given thanks, he broke it and gave it to his disciples, saying, "Take and eat; this is my body." Then he took a cup, and when he had given thanks, he gave it to them, saying, "Drink from it, all of you. This is my blood of the covenant, which is poured out for many for the forgiveness of sins. I tell you, I will not drink from this fruit of the vine from now on until that day when I drink it new with you in my Father's kingdom."

MATTHEW 26:26–29*

In health care, the nutritional status of a patient is an integral part of a clinical evaluation. Questions such as "How is your appetite?" or "When was your last meal?" are used in the evaluation. The purpose of such questions is to help the physician evaluate the nutritional status as a component of the health of the patient. A lack of appetite occurs commonly under stressful situations. This is related to a series of complex changes that occur in the brain and the hormonal system under stress. In other words, the human body does not recognize eating as a priority in stressful situations.

As it was getting closer to his crucifixion, Jesus was under a lot of stress. As far as I can tell, it is very unlikely that Jesus ate a whole meal the night of the Last Supper. He may have eaten a small piece of bread as he was leading the first Communion. This gives the Last Supper even more profound religious meaning, and it was a demonstration of Jesus' love for each one of us. But in terms of caloric intake, it was probably inconsequential or negligible.

The Agony in the Garden

And being in anguish, he prayed more earnestly, and his sweat
was like drops of blood falling to the ground.

Luke 22:44

After supper, Jesus and his disciples went to the Mount of Olives.
Jesus' agony in the garden fully expresses his human nature and shows
the conflict between his divine nature and human nature.

As the Son of God, Jesus was the ultimate prophet. He knew ahead
of time the brutality of the punishment he was about to suffer. Even in
his unique situation, he was not guessing or imagining things. As the
living God, his foreknowledge about his upcoming crucifixion was
beyond real. And yet that divine knowledge about the crucifixion had
to be handled by Jesus, the man. As his human brain received and
processed such an enormous amount of painful, detailed information
about the suffering that lay before him, his mind and body were overwhelmingly stressed.

Jesus' body reacted in a normal manner to the upcoming danger.
His stressed brain activated his hormonal system to prepare his body for
the upcoming battle. His heart rate and blood pressure increased in
response to the danger. These changes in the vital signs are the result of
the release of a group of hormones that together make up what is known
as the "fight-or-flight response." Examples of these substances include
adrenaline, noradrenaline, steroids, and endorphins. At this hormonal
stage, a person can respond to danger by running faster and by with-
standing significant levels of pain. We have all heard of times when someone responded to a crisis by performing a physical task that would have
been impossible at other times, and then wondered afterward how they
managed to do it.

The disciples who were with him at the garden had never seen him
so extremely disturbed. Luke portrayed the details of Jesus' time in the
Garden of Gethsemane, revealing his severe physical and emotional turmoil. Mel Gibson's movie, *The Passion of the Christ,* captured in detail the

drama at Gethsemane. It gave life to the Gospel of Luke as the actor portrayed Jesus' agony in the garden.

His suffering was of such magnitude that "his sweat was like drops of blood falling to the ground." This is a rare but real clinical condition called *hemohidrosis* or *hematidrosis* that occurs in moments of intensely overwhelming pain, stress, or shock. The smallest blood vessels (capillaries) of the sweat glands become very fragile and leak blood in the sweat glands, mixing the sweat with the blood.

There are other cases of *hematidrosis* described in human history. The great Leonardo Da Vinci mentioned a soldier who sweated blood prior to battle. More recently the *Indian Journal of Dermatology* described a case of a 72-year-old male whose undergarments became bloodstained in the abdominal area, especially in the morning, for approximately two months.[1]

The human response to physical and psychological stress is usually proportional to the severity of the potential danger. In other words, the more danger is perceived, the more acute and severe the hormonal response will be. Jesus' profound anguish is perfectly understandable from the clinical and psychological point of view. Nearly everyone has been in situations of danger, in which the body prepared itself for battle via the fight-or-flight response. Our human reaction is based on an educated guess about how bad the danger is going to be. Jesus did not have to make an educated guess about what was coming—he knew.

Jesus' body was ready for fight or flight. He was in significant amount of emotional distress. His human nature did not want to endure the extraordinary pain ahead of him, a perfectly normal human response. He prayed again to the Father: "Father, if you are willing, take this cup from me; yet not my will, but yours be done" (Luke 22:42).

These normal physical responses needed to be controlled in order for him to fulfill his mission. Jesus' answer to the extreme anguish was extreme praying.

THE TRIAL

Then the detachment of soldiers with its commander and the
Jewish officials arrested Jesus. They bound him and brought
him first to Annas, who was the father-in-law of Caiaphas, the
high priest that year.

JOHN 18:12–13

Anyone who has been interrogated understands that depositions,
trials, and anything to do with courts have the tendency to create a significant amount of stress. In modern times, most interrogations take
place in the morning or afternoon. The parties involved are usually represented by lawyers. It is a somewhat reasonable setup. Nevertheless, it
is energy-consuming and emotionally draining to be involved in any
trial, especially if a death sentence might be the end result.

Jesus' exposure to the justice system was very harsh. He was
removed from the Garden of Gethsemane late on Thursday night, and
early Friday morning, he was interrogated by religious and political leaders. Those leaders were trying to justify the death penalty for Jesus. Initially they thought that task would be easy, but it became more difficult
when the Roman prefect, Pontius Pilate, started hesitating when he could
not find anything that Jesus did wrong:

"What is truth?" retorted Pilate. With this he went out again to
the Jews gathered there and said, "I find no basis for a charge
against him."

JOHN 18:38

I'm sure that Pilate could sense the underlying jealousy against the
young, charismatic Jesus. The arguments were not enough to justify the
death penalty and even less sufficient to justify crucifixion.

During the multiple trips between the Jewish and Roman authorities,
Jesus was verbally and physically abused. He had not slept for at least
twenty-four hours, and the time of his last real meal is uncertain. The

scenario described above is enough to create extreme fatigue and an over-whelming nervous breakdown.

JESUS' TRIALS

From Thursday Evening to Friday Morning

- Jesus is arrested at the Garden of Gethsemane
- The inquiry before Annas
- The inquiry before Caiaphas (high priest)
- Jesus before the Sanhedrin
- The trial before Pilate at the praetorium
- Jesus before Herod
- Jesus before Pilate (2nd time)

John 18 – 19
Luke 22 – 23

The Jewish authorities realized that Pilate was hesitating about the

This map of the city summarizes Jesus' journey from the Upper Room to Calvary.

death sentence. At this point, they executed a very strong political maneuver by questioning Pilate's loyalty to Caesar: "From then on, Pilate tried to set Jesus free, but the Jewish leaders kept shouting, 'If you let this man go, you are no friend of Caesar. Anyone who claims to be a king opposes Caesar'" (John 19:12).

It is quite important to realize the implications of that accusation against a politician who was the representative of the Roman Empire in the region. In those days, there was a fine line between not being a friend of Caesar and being a traitor. Obviously, Pilate did not want to take the chance of being accused of something so close to treason. Therefore, he washed his hands of the innocent blood of Jesus. (Well, he thought he did.) In analyzing Pilate's actions, I try to keep in mind his social-political atmosphere. I think about politicians and non-politicians, and ask myself how many people would have done it differently. It is a scary thought. Sometimes, I feel that Pilate was just a politician in the wrong place and in the wrong time.

Finally, after a whole night of interrogations and presentation of false testimonies, Jesus was found guilty of blasphemy and condemned to the cross.

The Scourging

Then Pilate took Jesus and had him flogged.

JOHN 19:1

It is quite possible that some pre-crucifixion torture was an intrinsic component of all crucifixion proceedings. There is evidence that some victims died from the beatings alone. The brutal beating that took place as a preamble to the crucifixion could conceivably bring about death, especially if the victim was already weak or had some unrecognized illness.

Jesus was exposed to a very intense scourging. Some believe that Pilate wanted to impress the Jewish people with his sternness and thereby obtain a lighter punishment for Jesus: "Once more Pilate came out and said to the Jews gathered there, 'Look, I am bringing Him out to you to let you know that I find no basis for a charge against him'" (John 19:4).

The Romans used a whip called the flagrum.[2] It was loaded with destructive components such as pieces of metal, bones, animal teeth, and anything that could potentially cause damage to the victim's body.

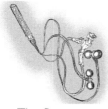

Each time the flagrum landed on Jesus' body, it created two types of injuries; superficial lacerations and deep-tissue bruises. The initial superficial lacerations became deeper and deeper as the punishment continued, and eventually the muscles from the back as well as the ribs became

The flagrum

exposed. This brings to mind the prophetic words of the psalm:

> Dogs surround me,
> a pack of villains encircles me;
> they pierce my hands and my feet. All my bones are on display;
> people stare and gloat over me.

PSALM 22:16–17

The expression "all my bones are on display" does not refer to Jesus being very thin or malnourished. Indeed, it is a very accurate representation of the damage to his back produced by the whip, to the point that his ribs and backbones were exposed.

This special whip also produced deep-tissue bruises that could account for a significant amount of bleeding in the muscles. Lacerations produce external bleeding, while the soft-tissue damage can result in blood being lost in the deep muscles, also called internal bleeding.

The final result of this barbaric scourging is extraordinary physical disfiguration. Long before the actual crucifixion, the prophet Isaiah wrote:

> Just as there were many who were appalled at him—
> his appearance was so disfigured beyond that of any human
> being
> and his form marred beyond human likeness....

ISAIAH 52:14

THE CROWN OF THORNS

> The soldiers twisted together a crown of thorns and put it on
> his head. They clothed him in a purple robe.

JOHN 19:2

The human scalp bleeds easily in cases of trauma to the head. Even small lacerations in the scalp can be source of torrential bleeding. The reason for this is that the scalp has an enormous number of blood vessels close to the surface; a doctor would say that it is extremely "vascular."

By the time Jesus received the crown of thorns, he had been exposed already to an enormous amount of physical and emotional trauma. He had not eaten or drunk anything substantial for a significant length of time. Most likely he was dehydrated even before losing the enormous amount of blood that flowed during his flogging. The combination of the uncontrolled blood loss and the lack of fluid intake created the state of *hypovolemia,* which means his blood volume was low.

The crown of sharp thorns placed on Jesus' head increased the already-significant blood loss from his body. The Roman soldiers continued to hit him in the head after the crown was in place. This cruel beating stimulated further hemorrhage: "[They] went up to him again and again, saying, 'Hail, king of the Jews!' And they slapped him in the face" (John 19:3). The crown of thorns covered the whole scalp instead of being the kind of crown which looks like an incomplete ring. The thorns measured one to two inches long.[3]

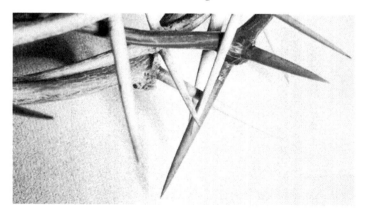

It is noteworthy to realize that the crown of thorns was not part of the ordinary crucifixion routine. It was unique to Jesus' crucifixion.

THE WAY OF THE CROSS

As the soldiers led him away, they seized Simon from Cyrene, who was on his way in from the country, and put the cross on him and made him carry it behind Jesus.

LUKE 23:26

In the old city of Jerusalem, there is a route that traditionally has been known as the route that took Jesus from the Roman fortress to the crucifixion site, also called Golgotha or "place of the skull." The route is called the Via Dolorosa or the "Way of Suffering." The distance of this traditional route is approximately six hundred meters or two thousand feet. (Some recent archeological findings question the currently accepted location of the Via Dolorosa.[4])

Regardless of the exact location of the streets, it is documented that Jesus had to walk from the Roman prefect's palace to Golgotha. It catches my attention that while the three Synoptic Gospels—Matthew, Mark, and Luke—mentioned that a Cyrenian named Simon was tapped to carry the cross for the convicted Jesus, John's Gospel does not mention him:

Finally Pilate handed him over to them to be crucified. So the soldiers took charge of Jesus. Carrying his own cross, he went out to the place of the Skull (which in Aramaic is called Golgotha).

JOHN 19:16–17

A few questions need to be addressed: (1) Did Jesus carry the whole cross, or did he carry the horizontal bar only? (2) Was he on a flat street or a hill? (3) How many times did he fall? (4) What did the Cyrenian man actually carry?

The whole interaction of the Cyrenian with Jesus is somewhat confusing, although the fact that he was mentioned in three out of the four Gospels seems to be enough evidence that someone named Simon was part of the journey on the Via Dolorosa.

It is a well-established fact that it would have been virtually impossible for one man to carry the whole cross. A distance of two thousand feet is too far to carry more than three hundred pounds,[5] especially for somebody who was already close to death from abuse and floggings. Jesus might have been able to carry the horizontal bar, the *patibulum,* for part of the distance. The horizontal bar weighed between eighty and one hundred ten pounds.[6] The Cyrenian might have helped him carry this horizontal bar by walking behind him, or he might have simply finished the route for a man who barely could walk.

Tradition says that Jesus fell three times. There is no biblical evidence of that number of falls, but due to his extreme fatigue, blood loss, dehydration, prolonged fasting, and extraordinary pain, it is quite possible that he fell not only three times but actually multiple times. Also, the route is rough and not particularly flat, especially coming down the steps of the palace.

Falls while carrying heavy objects on one's back carry intrinsic dangers. The momentum created by the fall can cause injuries similar to those of the impact of a steering wheel against the chest in a high-speed motor vehicle accident. Imagine a fall from the top of the steps of the palace with the horizontal bar of the cross on your back. The heart and lungs, trapped between two opposing forces, could suffer potentially lethal cardiac and pulmonary contusions. Cardiac contusions could subsequently lead to cardiac rupture. Some colleagues in the medical field believe that cardiac contusion followed by cardiac rupture might explain partially why Jesus' death was so fast.

Jesus carrying the horizontal bar of the cross.

The T-shaped cross used by the Romans.

CRUCIFIXION PROCEEDINGS

My mouth is dried up like a potsherd,
and my tongue sticks to the roof of my mouth;
you lay me in the dust of death.
Dogs surround me,
a pack of villains encircles me;
they pierce my hands and my feet.

PSALM 22:15–16

The rationale for using crucifixion as a mode of execution included two main goals. The first was to produce prolonged and extraordinary amount of pain. The second goal was to intimidate the population by presenting a barbaric public execution. The message was meant to be intimidating: "This could happen to you if you defy the Roman Empire."

Jesus was the most innocent person who ever faced this death penalty. Even Pilate thought so. He said, "You brought me this man as one who was inciting the people to rebellion. I have examined him in your presence and have found no basis for your charges against him"

(Luke 23:13–14). Despite Pilate's intent to release him, the political pressure that the Jewish leaders placed on him was too much for him. Pilate sentenced Jesus to death on a cross.

On foot, Jesus was taken to a place on the outskirts of the city named the Skull (Golgotha in Hebrew) to be crucified. This location had been specially chosen to allow a public view of the executions that took place there. Presumably, the location was also important from a public health perspective, due to the fact that some of the crucified, dead bodies remained on their crosses for a while, for added gruesome intimidation.

As previously mentioned, the Romans had perfected the art of crucifixion. They dedicated skilled soldiers to this particular task. The placement of the nails had to be precise in order to both keep the body secured to the cross and to generate the greatest amount of pain. Some basic but practical knowledge of anatomy must have been part of the training for these Roman soldiers.

Jesus' arms were secured to the cross by driving nails that were up to seven inches long and about three eighths of an inch thick right through his wrists.[7] Those nails were driven between the bones of his wrists. An important nerve, the median nerve, passes toward the hand there, and the nail would have damaged it, which would have caused his hands to bend into a claw-like position.[8] Worst of all, the damage to the nerve would have created severe cramps that travelled up through his arms to his shoulders. Those cramps are very painful, and they destroy the control and strength of the arms. Further, the body weight of a crucified person pulls the arms down, creating dislocation of the elbow and shoulder. It is not unusual for a victim of crucifixion to gain a couple of inches in the length of his arms.

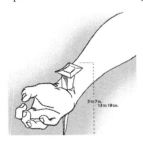

Characteristic claw hand created when the nail pierces the wrist.

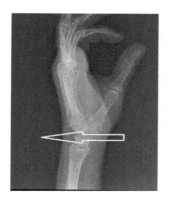 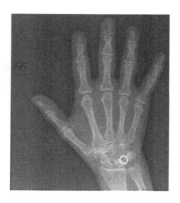

Hand X-rays reveal the pathway of the nail between the wrist bones.

Jesus' feet were then nailed to the "stipe," the upright part of the cross. Nails were driven through his feet between the second and third metatarsal bones, almost at the center of the foot. This particular location holds fast even when the weight of the person's body sags. There was initial bleeding due to damage to the arterial branches located between the metatarsals, but this bleeding was self-limiting since the nail itself as well as the weight of the body compressed the artery against the nail.

His knees were rotated outwardly and bent. The position created by this maneuver was extremely awkward and uncomfortable. The position of the victim on a cross creates an unprecedented amount of suffering. (Somehow, other human beings were capable of designing such a torture.) Once in a while, the soldiers would use a tiny seat to assist in supporting the body during the agony of death. (Why not add minimal "comfort"?) Let's not assume that providing this small seat was an act of mercy. It only served to prolong the torture for the victim. There is nothing merciful in crucifixion.

SLOW AND PAINFUL DEATH

We need to keep in mind that by the time Jesus was nailed to the cross, he already had lost a significant amount of blood due to the abusive and barbaric flogging he had suffered a few hours earlier. He had not eaten for a long time. He was already very weak and critically injured.

In order to understand what happened next, it is important to know how it is that we humans breathe. People breathe using a combination of muscles that work in a synchronized fashion, opposite from each other. One group of muscles contracts while the other group relaxes and vice versa. This automatic, well-synchronized system allows the chest wall to expand for inspiration and to contract in size for expiration. The lungs are inside the chest cavity in what is called the pleural space. The inspiratory and expiratory movements allow the air to get in and out of the lungs by creating negative and positive pressure inside the pleural space.

When somebody is crucified, a cascade of events gets triggered. The victim's body dies slowly by degrees and every moment is excruciatingly painful. Since the body has been suspended from only three fixed points, the two wrists and the feet together, placing weight on any point creates enormous pain. Instinctively, the victim alternates his weight between his wrists and feet. Each time the victim relaxes, his body drops by gravity and starts dislocating the joints of his upper extremities. As I mentioned earlier, by the time of death it was not unusual for the person's arms to gain a few inches in length due to the dislocation of the elbows and shoulders. The end result of the stretched and dislocated arms is that the whole chest wall is pulled outward and upward, fixing the chest in full inhalation. This particular derangement affects the respiratory dynamics in a very negative way.

The end result of this horrible and awkward position is that areas of the lung start to collapse, impairing the gas exchange. The oxygen in blood and tissues decline while the poisonous carbon dioxide (CO_2) builds up. In medical terminology, the cross produces respiratory failure by suffocation.[9]

In addition, the heart is profoundly affected by suffocation. You may have heard the term "cardio-respiratory system." This term recognizes the fact that the lungs and the heart are functionally related. The lungs are responsible for obtaining the oxygen from the air while eliminating the carbon dioxide, and the circulatory system is responsible for the delivery of the oxygen to the tissues along with the delivery of the toxic carbon dioxide from the tissues to the lungs where it can be eliminated. If one fails, the other one eventually fails. The only question is when.

The respiratory failure (suffocation) produces heart failure. One of the consequences of heart failure is the accumulation of fluid in the tissues and body cavities, which is known as edema and effusions. An effusion is a detrimental accumulation of fluid in a body cavity. There can be pulmonary edema (fluid inside the lung tissue), or edema in the lower extremities, or fluid in the pleural cavity (pleural effusion) or pericardial cavity (pericardial effusion), or in any other body cavity.

A normal, healthy adult would try to overcome his compromised respiratory system by putting his weight on his pierced feet and pushing himself upward in order to bring his shoulders down to the level of the rib cage. From the respiratory standpoint, this action is intended to regain a more favorable position. A person could try to do this maneuver as long as and as often as he could withstand the pain in his feet. Once the pain became unbearable, he would then drop down again until he could catch a breath. This agonizing cycle would repeat again and again.

For young, healthy individuals, the process of dying on the cross could take between two to four days. The healthier and stronger an individual was to begin with, the longer he could withstand the punishment. The final result was the same: death. But a strong man would die a very slow death indeed.

HASTENING THE END

Sometimes during a lengthy crucifixion, the soldiers as well as the spectators would get tired of watching the ordeal. Because healthy, muscular victims could temporarily overcome the respiratory unbalance by pushing their bodies upward, the Roman soldiers would fracture the victim's legs with a hard blow, to counteract this survival maneuver and to speed up the dying process. Once the legs were broken, the victim could not overcome the respiratory nightmare and would succumb to suffocation.

According to the Gospel of John, the soldiers broke the legs of the other two victims who were crucified alongside Jesus. But Jesus did not need to have his legs broken: "The soldiers therefore came and broke the legs of the first man who had been crucified with Jesus, and then those of the other. But when they came to Jesus and found that he was already dead, they did not break his legs" (John 19:32–33).

According to the Gospel of Mark, Jesus and his cross mates were placed on their crosses at nine o'clock in the morning. By three o'clock in the afternoon, Jesus was dead (see Mark 15:25–37).

The other two victims were still alive by the time Jesus died. Because it was almost time for the Jewish Passover to begin, it was imperative to make sure that there would be no bodies hanging on crosses by the solemn Sabbath of that week. For this reason, the soldiers proceeded to break the legs of the other two victims to hasten their deaths.

The fact that Jesus' two cross mates had to have their legs broken implies that they were not exposed to the same barbaric punishment that Jesus was. They were not flogged as hard as Jesus was, or maybe they were not flogged at all. If Jesus' cross mates were not flogged at all, then we might assume that flogging was not even a standard part of the proceedings. Obviously, they were in better physical shape by the time the three were crucified together. Why was their degree of punishment less severe than what Jesus suffered? Jesus' flogging was so intense that he nearly died from it. As I mentioned earlier, it could be related to Pilate's failed effort to placate the Jews and thereby to get a lesser penalty for Jesus. Pilate presented Jesus to the Jews after the intense flogging as a last attempt to gain a lesser penalty for him. It did not work; Jesus' fate had been established already:

> ...knowing it was out of self-interest that the chief priests had handed Jesus over to him. But the chief priests stirred up the crowd to have Pilate release Barabbas instead.
>
> "What shall I do, then, with the one you call the king of the Jews?" Pilate asked them.
>
> "Crucify him!" they shouted.

MARK 15:10–13

Four different versions of the Passion (the sufferings of Jesus at the time of his crucifixion) appear in each of the four Gospels (Matthew, Mark, Luke, and John). Each one of them focuses on different aspects of the ordeal. We can also appreciate the different styles of the authors. Between the four of them, the Gospels provide a chronology of the events surrounding Jesus' last hours. Yet from a medical standpoint, most of the information regarding Jesus' physical suffering is found in the book of Isaiah and in Psalm 22, which describes his suffering in a very detailed way.

> I am poured out like water,
>> and all my bones are out of joint.
> My heart has turned to wax;
>> it has melted within me.
> My mouth is dried up like a potsherd,
>> and my tongue sticks to the roof of my mouth;
>> you lay me in the dust of death.
> Dogs surround me,
>> a pack of villains encircles me;
>> they pierce my hands and my feet.
> All my bones are on display;
>> people stare and gloat over me.

They divide my clothes among them
and cast lots for my garment.

PSALM 22:15–18

In this psalm, which is considered prophetic of Jesus' death on the cross, we see the description of dislocated bones and severe dehydration ("my tongue sticks to the roof of my mouth"). A sticky, dry tongue is a classic sign of dehydration. The psalm also describes the piercing of the hands and feet, and also refers to the exposed bones that resulted from the ruthless flogging that Jesus received prior to being nailed to the cross. His state of overwhelming fatigue and even heart failure is insinuated by the expressions, "I am poured out like water.... My heart has turned to wax; it has melted within me."

JESUS' DEATH

Jesus called out with a loud voice, "Father, into your hands I commit my spirit." When he said this, he breathed his last.

LUKE 23:46

I have previously discussed the goals of crucifixion as an execution method. One of the goals was to inflict a substantial amount of pain over a prolonged length of time—we are talking about *days*. It is quite obvious that Jesus' case was different in terms of his length of time on the cross, as he was only hanging on the cross for approximately six hours. In fact, Pilate acted surprised when he found out that he was already dead:

Joseph of Arimathea, a prominent member of the Council, who was himself waiting for the kingdom of God, went boldly to Pilate and asked for Jesus' body. Pilate was surprised to hear that he was already dead. Summoning the centurion, he asked him if Jesus had already died.

MARK 15:43–44

A legitimate question is why Jesus' death was so fast. I am using the word "fast" carefully because time is relative when the victim is on the cross; seconds appear like minutes, minutes like hours, and hours like days. Nevertheless, crucifixion victims usually linger much longer than Jesus did.

The mechanism of death on the cross is suffocation, but a key variable in Jesus' case was the overwhelming flogging that preceded his time on the cross itself. That flogging resulted in such extraordinary loss of blood that his low blood volume state, or hypovolemic shock, sped up the already lethal cascade of consequences. As shock-trauma specialists well know, hypovolemic shock plus respiratory derangements can be a dangerous combination. Jesus had that combination.

In simple terms, Jesus' cardiorespiratory system could not provide oxygenated blood to the tissues of his body. On one hand, the ability of his lungs to obtain the oxygen from the air was seriously affected. On the other hand, he did not have enough blood left in his body to deliver the poorly oxygenated blood to his tissues.

This double derangement produces an accumulation of acid in all the tissues of the body. The heart muscle is very particular in terms of its oxygen requirements. Suffice it to say that bad things happen when the heart is not getting enough oxygen. More specifically, you can expect malignant cardiac arrhythmias, myocardial infarction, and overwhelming heart failure. The term "malignant cardiac arrhythmias" refers to abnormal heart rhythms that might impair the pumping function of the heart and have a lethal potential. "Myocardial infarction" is better known as a heart attack, when an area of the heart muscle is deprived of oxygen, producing cardiac muscle death. The heart attack itself can stimulate malignant arrhythmias or damage so much cardiac muscle that it affects the pump function of the heart, resulting in heart failure. It implies a weak heart that is failing to meet the oxygenated blood requirement of the person's body.

In summary, despite the fact that the primary mechanism of death in a crucified victim is suffocation, Jesus had other compounding factors that would have accelerated his death.[10]

THE BLOOD AND THE WATER

Now it was the day of Preparation, and the next day was to be a special Sabbath. Because the Jewish leaders did not want the bodies left on the crosses during the Sabbath, they asked Pilate to have the legs broken and the bodies taken down. The soldiers therefore came and broke the legs of the first man who had been crucified with Jesus, and then those of the other. But when they came to Jesus and found that he was already dead, they did not break his legs. Instead, one of the soldiers pierced Jesus' side with a spear, bringing a sudden flow of blood and water.

JOHN 19:31–34

When I was a child, I was puzzled by the above description. The whole thing about water coming out of the chest was mysterious to me. Later on, I learned about some of the religious symbolism of the mix of blood and water; the theological interpretation of the water pouring out of Jesus' chest is tied into baptism.

The first time that I heard the medical explanation of the water pouring out of the chest was during my time in medical school. I read the book *A Doctor at Calvary,* in which the author, Dr. Barbet, gave a possible explanation for the water, stating that Jesus might have developed a pericardial effusion.[11] More recently, some articles in medical literature have provided more insight regarding this issue. It is well-established in the medical community that heart failure produces watery effusions. From the medical standpoint, heart failure makes a lot of sense as the culprit for the development of the effusions that helped to kill Jesus because every mechanism for the development of pleural and pericardial effusions was in place in Jesus' body.

Why did both water and blood come out when the soldier's spear pierced his side? The lance would have gone through several layers of tissue before hitting the right side of the heart, either the right atrium or right ventricle, depending on the cardiac and respiratory movements. The layers include: skin, subcutaneous tissue, chest wall muscle, pleura, pleural cavity, pericardium, pericardial cavity, and then the right chambers of the heart. As you can see in Fig. 11, once the lance hit the pleural cavity and then the pericardial cavity, water would start to drain, but it would be overpowered by the brisk rush of blood that would gush out of the heart. The right chambers of the heart are the most likely to be injured by stab wounds entering the chest through the front. In other words, they are the closest parts of the heart to the chest wall.

The bleeding from a stab wound to the chest is usually very intense. The blood comes out under pressure and it does have a very strong visual impact for any bystander. In the case of Jesus, we know the certain identity of at least two bystanders who were close enough to the cross and standing at the appropriate angle that would allow them to witness this hemorrhage. We know that John, the "beloved disciple," was so close because Jesus spoke to him and gave him a very unique and specific assignment: to take care of his mother, Mary:

When Jesus saw his mother there, and the disciple whom he loved standing nearby, he said to her, "Woman, here is your son," and to the disciple, "Here is your mother." From that time on, this disciple took her into his home.

JOHN 19:26–27

It is noteworthy that John's Gospel is the only one that mentions the blood and the water. It does make sense. He was the disciple who was able to withstand the fear of being arrested and prosecuted by the Romans. His love for his leader was stronger than fear and he placed himself in the front row, accompanying Jesus' sorrowful mother.

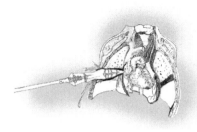 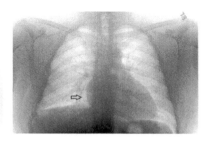

Trajectory of the spear   Chest X-ray showing entry point

STRANGE REACTION OF MOTHER NATURE

At noon, darkness came over the whole land until three in the afternoon. And at three in the afternoon Jesus cried out in a loud voice, "Eloi, Eloi, lema sabachthani?" (which means "My God, my God, why have you forsaken me?").

MARK 15:33–34

Reading the Gospels' accounts of the Crucifixion can be overwhelming in terms of the amount of information presented. For that reason, I had never paid too much attention to the strange and mysterious natural events that occurred during Jesus' last hours. It was as if Mother Nature, God's created earth, was making some strong statements during those hours surrounding Jesus' death.

Can you imagine the overwhelming fear that would have been felt by the witnesses when they saw darkness—at noon? The three Synoptic Gospels mentioned the darkness that took everybody by surprise. Luke is the most specific, using the word "eclipse" to describe this strange sight:

It was now about noon and darkness came over the whole land until three in the afternoon because of an eclipse of the sun. Then the veil of the temple was torn down the middle.

LUKE 23:44–45

It gets even more strange. Matthew shares about the noontime darkness in the land and also goes on to describe other even more mysterious developments:

> At that moment the curtain of the temple was torn in two from top to bottom. The earth shook, the rocks split and the tombs broke open. The bodies of many holy people who had died were raised to life. They came out of the tombs after Jesus' resurrection and went into the holy city and appeared to many people.

MATTHEW 27:51–53

Matthew, Mark, and Luke all mention the tearing of the sanctuary veil. They were very specific about stating that it was torn from top to bottom, down the middle. But the only one who mentions the earthquake is Matthew. When I first read this, I was tempted to explain the tear in the veil as a consequence of the earthquake, but the tear happened *prior* to the quake if we follow Matthew's sequence word by word. The curtain itself was much taller than human height and woven to be immensely thick—in other words, nearly impossible to tear.

It is true that eclipses and earthquakes are both natural phenomena that are known to occur; no question about it. But how often do they occur in the same day—and not only within the same twenty-four hours, but almost simultaneously? The statistical likelihood of these two major events happening at the same time is very small. In modern days, an eclipse of any kind is not scary because we have been warned ahead of time, and we find these events to be unique to watch—an experience of a lifetime. However, in the first century, there was no way of broadcasting a warning about an upcoming eclipse. And an eclipse of the sun that just "happened" at that historical moment, just when an innocent young man who some believed was the Son of God was being crucified, would have been an extremely frightening experience.

In my personal experience, I have witnessed several low-scale earthquakes. These particular earthquakes did not damage anything, but from my point of view, they were very scary. I find earthquakes to be scarier than hurricanes, which I have also experienced in the Dominican Republic. In an earthquake, the vibration of the land creates a very disturbing sound wave that threatens impending doom. The earthquakes that I have been exposed to would be considered mild. I cannot imagine being in a big one like the one the day Jesus died, capable of splitting rocks in a half.

Let us reconstruct the story. Jesus, the man who was believed to be the Son of God, was placed on the cross at nine o'clock in the morning. Three hours later, at noon, darkness came over the whole land, and it lasted for three hours. At the moment he breathed his last, the curtain of the temple tore in half, without any natural explanation. An earthquake followed that was strong enough to split rocks in half. Righteous people rose out of their tombs and moved around the city.

Even the pagan soldiers were convinced that by crucifying Jesus, they had just killed the Son of God:

When the centurion and those with him who were guarding Jesus saw the earthquake and all that had happened, they were terrified, and exclaimed, "Surely he was the Son of God!"

MATTHEW 27:54

Besides mentioning the centurion's reaction, the Gospel of Luke also mentions how the rest of the bystanders reacted to the natural events:

The centurion, seeing what had happened, praised God and said, "Surely this was a righteous man." When all the people who had gathered to witness this sight saw what took place, they beat their breasts and went away. But all those who knew him, including the women who had followed him from Galilee, stood at a distance, watching these things.

LUKE 23:47–49

How can anybody fail to be convinced by this unprecedented (and never since repeated) cluster of natural and supernatural events that appear to have been orchestrated around the agony Jesus was enduring?

When I referred to the star of Bethlehem earlier, I mentioned Kepler's contribution to astronomy. The same method can be used to determine the sky map during Pontius Pilate's time. It appears as though there was in fact a lunar eclipse on April 3, AD 33, most likely the day of the cross.[12] So let us add this reddish moon (bloody moon) rising after dark. The whole cluster of phenomena was overwhelming, and the connection to Jesus' suffering is very clear.

JOHN'S TESTIMONY

The man who saw it has given testimony, and his testimony is true. He knows that he tells the truth, and he testifies so that you also may believe. These things happened so that the scripture would be fulfilled: "Not one of his bones will be broken."

JOHN 19:35–36

I have read about and listened to the story of the Passion of the Christ according to John so many times. But I have to say that John's testimony continues to have a strong effect on me, and it has since I was a little boy. I remember the first time I heard it. It was Holy Friday and, as was traditional in my family, we went to church. The Catholic Church has celebrated Holy Friday the same way for hundreds of years. The whole Passion story according to John is read from beginning to end in a very solemn way. Three lectors—three voices—take turns reading the words. Each one is assigned a person. For example, the celebrating priest reads anything pertaining to Jesus, the co-celebrant reads about everybody else besides Jesus, and a third person serves as the narrator.

From the first time I heard the account of the Passion, I was overwhelmed by Jesus' suffering and the unfairness of the ordeal. And even that first time, this line caught my ear: "The man who saw it has given testimony" (John 19:35). My reaction when I was young was, "What?

What was that?" Ever since then, I have always paid significant attention to this particular line. I call it an *h-mail,* or "historical mail." Every time I hear it, it sounds to me as though John has traveled from the past to tell us that he was there, he saw everything, and, most importantly, he has no reason to mislead us.

One thing I know is that you can remove this paragraph and the sequence of the reading will not be affected. In other words, the story has already been told without this particular paragraph. So what is the meaning of this segment? Why did John feel the need to add this? This is a question that deserves our attention. In fact, we can't find another testimony like this in the Bible. It is unique. So consider the author. Knowing the author's background provides insight on the piece and allows the reader to better capture or understand the message.

John was one of the twelve disciples who followed Jesus. He was James' younger brother, and their father's name was Zebedee. His mother, Salome, was Mary's youngest sister. James and John were Jesus' cousins. As it was customary in those times that the sons would help their father in his job, James and John became fishermen like their father. After Jesus called them to follow him, they became part of his inner circle. In fact, along with Peter, James and John were the ones who witnessed the transfiguration of Jesus as well as the miracle of the daughter of Jairus, whom he raised from the dead.

It appears as though John and James had an interesting mix of personalities. On one hand, they were very calm and gentle, but when their patience was pushed to its limits, their anger became thunderous. Jesus named them "Boanerges" or "sons of thunder" (Mark 3:17). Most of us know someone who is like that: generally gentle but explosive when patience runs out. For me, it is important to be able to compare these biblical characters to people today; in spite of the passage of centuries, they are very similar. Jesus was able to see beyond John's explosiveness. He could see his heart, and he could tell that his good heart made him trustworthy.

Jesus was so close to him that he asked him to take care of his mother in his final hours, the kind of request that is only given to a very special, trusted, and beloved person. Remember that whereas most of the disciples stood at a distance during Jesus' ordeal on the cross (or went into hiding), John demonstrated his love and loyalty to Jesus by staying by his side, accompanying Mary. John was so close to Jesus that he is known as "the beloved disciple." Throughout their years under Jesus' mentorship, both John and James blossomed as disciples, becoming key members of the group.

Then during Jesus' last hours, this beloved disciple stood beside Mary, overwhelmed by what was happening and, what was worse, unable to do anything. Surely he realized that he had just witnessed the most important event in the history of humanity: the Son of God's crucifixion. The most innocent man had been executed by the most barbaric method known. He must have realized that what he had just witnessed would change the whole world forever. He felt responsible for his role as an eye-witness so future generations would believe that the story described by him was truth.

I ask you; is he a reliable witness? Knowing what we do about his personality, see what he said:

> Now it was the day of Preparation, and the next day was to be a special Sabbath. Because the Jewish leaders did not want the bodies left on the crosses during the Sabbath, they asked Pilate to have the legs broken and the bodies taken down. The soldiers therefore came and broke the legs of the first man who had been crucified with Jesus, and then those of the other. But when they came to Jesus and found that he was already dead, they did not break his legs. Instead, one of the soldiers pierced Jesus' side with a spear, bringing a sudden flow of blood and water. *The man who saw it has given testimony, and his testimony is true. He knows that he tells the truth, and he testifies so that you also may believe.*

JOHN 19:31–35, EMPHASIS ADDED

CHAPTER 5

THE RESURRECTION

Early on the first day of the week, while it was still dark, Mary Magdalene went to the tomb and saw that the stone had been removed from the entrance. So she came running to Simon Peter and the other disciple, the one Jesus loved, and said, "They have taken the Lord out of the tomb, and we don't know where they have put him!"

So Peter and the other disciple started for the tomb. Both were running, but the other disciple outran Peter and reached the tomb first. He bent over and looked in at the strips of linen lying there but did not go in. Then Simon Peter came along behind him and went straight into the tomb. He saw the strips of linen lying there, as well as the cloth that had been wrapped around Jesus' head. The cloth was still lying in its place, separate from the linen. Finally the other disciple, who had reached the tomb first, also went inside. He saw and believed. (They still did not understand from Scripture that Jesus had to rise from the dead.)

JOHN 20:1–9

Up to this point, we have talked about a marvelous leader who was crucified under the accusation of blasphemy. The reality is that Jesus was somewhat intimidating to the establishment at that time. He was becoming too popular among the poor people and the Gentiles. Jesus was the kind of leader whose words and actions were fused together, and that can be powerful and intimidating.

Eliminating the head of a movement is one way of disabling any unwanted political, religious, or social movement. But sometimes this particular maneuver cannot control what has already started and in fact can make it worse. It appears that after his death, Jesus continued to be a problem for the social, political, and religious establishment. Actually, it probably became a bigger problem—a nightmare.

For the first time, a man had been killed on the cross, and three days later his body had disappeared from its tomb—a tomb that was heavily guarded by the imperial forces. Even more unusual, some rumors started to spread around Jerusalem that Jesus had been seen alive, bearing the obvious marks of the crucifixion ordeal. Could it be that the leader they had executed had come back to life? Could it have happened as he himself had predicted? He had gathered his disciples to tell them something: "He said to them, 'The Son of Man is going to be delivered into the hands of men. They will kill him, and on the third day he will be raised to life.' And the disciples were filled with grief" (Matthew 17:22–23).

In the history of humanity, there have been numerous other influential religious leaders. Some of them have played a very important role in shaping human history. But, except Jesus, no one else had ever said that he was capable of being resurrected—and then had proved it.

If the story about Jesus had ended at his death, then what would be the difference between him and any other great leader or martyr? The answer is no difference. It would have been just another tragedy. It is the Resurrection that sets Jesus apart from any other influential religious leader. Jesus' story is incomplete if we do not address the events that happened after his death.

Being perceived as reliable or trustworthy is paramount in any influential leader, especially a religious one. Throughout human history, important religious figures (whether Christian or not) *must* be reliable and trustworthy. Their followers must find them worthy of their confidence. Jesus is not the exception to this rule. He was very particular about the truth.

He proved how important the truth was for him by the way he responded to his enemies. Just consider: a simple lie could have saved his life. He only needed to say "That was not what I meant," and he could have avoided the cross. But he did not change his testimony. He was fully aware of the fact that he was at his highest moment as a religious figure. People found his presence so extraordinary that they were calling him the Messiah. Then why would he put in jeopardy his credibility and reputation by promising to do something that he could not do? Why did he put himself into such an awkward position and take the risk of getting into the history not as a martyr but as a liar?

This particular line of reasoning is very important to keep in mind because the Resurrection is what makes Jesus unique, and when the Resurrection is analyzed, two conflicting positions emerge: real fact versus impossible fact, or Christians versus Rationalists. No one else had ever dared to claim that they could come back to life three days after dying. Obviously, no one else could have offered a promise like that. But the question remains: Did he actually do that? Is it true? Or is the Resurrection a myth—the result of the unresolved grief of his very close group of followers, or a lie perpetuated for the purpose of elevating the teachings of a great and unique leader?

This line of questioning is extremely important for believers and also for nonbelievers. If the Resurrection didn't happen, then billions of people have been following an extraordinary lie. This would have to be a very carefully orchestrated fraud to include a missing body and the testimony of more than five hundred people who declared they had seen him alive soon after he rose from the grave. Some of these witnesses were so certain of their own testimony about this that they themselves became martyrs.

It should be said that the implication of assuming that the Resurrection is a fraud is that there is nothing beyond death. If we say that Jesus did not come back to life, that the whole thing is a myth, we eliminate the strongest evidence that life is possible after death.

THEORIES AGAINST THE RESURRECTION

Let's go deeper into the arguments surrounding Jesus' resurrection. There are some different theories by which people who assume that Jesus was not resurrected try to explain the missing body.

Cadaver Hidden by the Disciples

According to this argument, Jesus and his disciples plotted ahead of time that Jesus' body was to be stolen and hidden. Later, they would pretend that he had risen from the dead as he had promised. By performing this fraud, they hoped to be able to keep his myth alive and to perpetuate it throughout the coming generations.

The only thing in favor of this theory is that frauds were, are, and will be part of human history. Frauds can be plausible enough to work. But there are several pitfalls with this particular theory. Let us start with something very simple. Looking at the background and character of Jesus and his disciples, it is easy to conclude that Jesus had no record of being a fraudulent man. There is no evidence of his lying in any other circumstances. Jesus can be considered a holy man and a good man regardless of whether or not you believe he was the Messiah. Quite simply, lying is not a quality of a holy man.

The other possibility was that the disciples stole the body due to their grief or simply to create chaos, and that Jesus was not involved in that decision, that this decision was made after his death by his close followers. Again, a background character check of these fishermen shows they were not sophisticated individuals, nor were they troublemakers who would have been incapable of doing such a task. Keep in mind that the tomb was under surveillance by well-trained, well-armed Roman guards; formidable soldiers were guarding Jesus' tomb. In order to steal that body, the disciples themselves would have needed to be mercenary soldiers with superior training. Obviously, this was not the case.

Another important factor to consider is that Jesus did not resist being arrested. He did not defend himself against the accusations. Think about this for a minute. It is understandable that he wanted to avoid any chaotic violence during his arrest that could end in injuries and the death of some of his followers. And then he failed to defend himself went he was put on trial. Keeping in mind that Jesus was very sharp and a very good speaker, we know that he could have held his ground in court, without a doubt. It appears as though getting out of this one alive was not his goal. The only explanation for his actions is that he had a bigger goal: immortality. It is fair to say that the theory that the disciples stole Jesus' body does not withstand any serious or basic logical scrutiny.

Cadaver Hidden by the Jewish and Romans Authorities

This second theory is related to the first one in the sense that it implies a fraud. In this case, the players are reversed. In this theory, the Roman and Jewish authorities performed a preemptive maneuver by hiding the body so it could not be stolen by Jesus' followers. The goal was to prevent the spread of a resurrection rumor. This particular theory would have been an extraordinary blow to Jesus' followers and would have stopped the growth of the Christian faith before it even got underway.

Imagine that indeed the Roman and Jewish authorities took possession of the body. It is safe to say that the story would have ended with a public display of the dead body that would have terminated the resurrection rumor so that Jesus' followers would give up and go back home.

But if they took the body in an attempt to nip a resurrection rumor in the bud, it certainly didn't work. It didn't work because they did not have that body, either.

It is interesting that there are rationalists who actually believe in this particular theory. They believe that Jesus' dead body is still hidden rather than resurrected. They believe any explanation is more plausible than resurrection. But one thing that none of them can explain is why, if they had it, the authorities did not put the body on display. It just does not make sense. Displaying the cadaver would have been the end of the movement and the end of a myth. So, why didn't they use that preemptive deterrent if they could have? Why not show the body and terminate once and for all the movement that was getting out of hand? It just doesn't add up.

The Women Went to the Wrong Tomb

So Joseph bought some linen cloth, took down the body, wrapped it in the linen, and placed it in a tomb cut out of rock. Then he rolled a stone against the entrance of the tomb. Mary Magdalene and Mary the mother of Joseph saw where he was laid.

MARK 15:46–47

The women who had come with Jesus from Galilee followed Joseph and saw the tomb and how his body was laid in it. Then they went home and prepared spices and perfumes. But they rested on the Sabbath in obedience to the commandment.

LUKE 23:55–56

Starting with the Gospels of Mark and Luke, we see that the location of the burial was clearly established public knowledge, or at least it was known by Jesus' followers. As described in Mark and Luke, the tomb was located close by the crucifixion site, and the women saw exactly where the body of the Lord was placed.

Keep in mind that the city of Jerusalem was not complex during those times. The tomb was located near the crucifixion site, a place located in highly visible area, and it is safe to say that getting lost was very unlikely, no matter how dark it was. Also consider that the ladies went back to tell the disciples the day after the Sabbath, and the men came running to check the empty tomb. Did they also go to the wrong place? Again, it is very unlikely. They knew where he had been buried.

We also should keep in mind that crucifixion proceedings were all about intimidation. There was nothing private about them. It was a public ordeal from beginning to end. Displaying the dead bodies was part of the scare tactics of the Romans. The highly visible location of the tomb for this so-called enemy of the establishment was not a state secret. In fact, considering that guards were posted there, the location could be considered part of the intimidation.

The Theory of the Faint

The term "theory" refers to a proposed explanation of empirical phenomena. It refers to the act of trying to explain phenomena. It does not imply testing of the possible explanation. With the multiple *theories* of disproving the Resurrection, people are trying to explain the empty tomb with anything that could explain the absent body, but they are leaving out of the analysis important variables. Objective substantiation is missing from these theories.

Take, for example, the theory of the faint, which is actually a funny one. This theory suggests that while Jesus was on the cross, he fainted. The Romans thought he was dead, so they allowed Joseph of Arimathea to take him down from the cross and lay him in the tomb. Once Jesus was in the tomb, he woke up because of the extreme cold of the tomb. He was injured, but strong enough to escape by moving the huge, heavy stone.

But an important detail was not taken into consideration when this theory was created. This is what the eyewitness John has to say about Jesus' last hour: "One of the soldiers pierced Jesus' side with a spear, bringing a sudden flow of blood and water" (John 19:34). John is describing a lethal injury. In order to bring "a sudden flow of blood and water," the lance would have to pass through the pleural space, then the pericardial space, and finally the right side of the heart, either the right atrium or the right ventricle. Let's define these anatomical terms. The pleural space refers to the cavity occupied by the lungs, and the pericardial space is the cavity where the heart is located. The right atrium and ventricle are the two chambers of the heart located anteriorly (in front of the heart). Most cardiac stab wounds affect the right chambers because of their location. Besides massive bleeding, this type of wound also allows air to get into the chest cavity, more specifically into the pleural space, and this causes the lungs to collapse because of the increased pressure inside the chest (thorax). This phenomenon is called pneumothorax. A pneumothorax is a dangerous condition that requires immediate attention lest it become lethal. A cardiac laceration secondary to a lance provokes a similar urgent medical crisis. A cardiac laceration can produce such massive bleeding that extraordinary and efficient medical attention is required to save the victim's life. Even in today's trauma settings, lacerations to the heart put the victim at high risk for death.

Even if by some chance Jesus fainted while on the cross, that lance would have sealed his death. It would have finished the job. He would not have been brought down from the cross alive. There is no way, Jose. It would be a virtual impossibility from the medical stand point.

Indirectly, this theory also accepts or implies that Jesus had some supernatural powers. Think about this: If, even after the man Jesus lost so much blood from the scourging, the crown of thorns, the crucifixion, and finally from a full-size lance making a hole in his heart, he was still able to revive well enough to move aside the heavy rock that blockaded him into the tomb, that is supernatural power!

The Theory of the Twin Brother

This theory really surprised me. Jesus had a twin brother?

It reminds me of the movie *The Prestige.* This movie is about a battle between two magicians. Each one of them wants to be the best. They push the envelope in terms of their tricks and stunts, each time performing tricks that are more and more complex. One of the magicians has an identical twin brother, which allows him to do some "impossible" stunts that are not logical in the other magician's mind. At the end, one of the brothers sacrifices his life to benefit the other one.

While the twin theory might be excellent for the plot of a Hollywood movie, I don't think we can buy it when it comes to disproving Jesus' resurrection. In fact, I find it somewhat admirable to hear someone say, "I can't explain the missing body. I don't know what happened with it, but resurrection is out of the question. I simply cannot believe that." In fact, I respect that. But what I find disturbing is the way some rationalists try to explain Jesus' missing body.

Respectable theories can only be created after a profound analysis of key information. If important information gets left out in the process of elaborating the theory, you have a weak theory. To explain the empty tomb, the "shotgun" approach appears to have been used. I remember hearing so many times in college, "If you don't know the answer, just say, 'I don't know.'" Later on when I became a physician, I could see even more clearly how important it is to say "I don't know" as I witnessed the fiascos of residents in conferences who were trying to make up answers to compensate for things they did not know. (Actually, it can be very entertaining.) It is important to be able to say "I don't know"; for a physician it can mean saving somebody's life.

The bottom line is that there is no documentation whatsoever that Jesus ever had an identical twin brother. For this theory to be true, two Jesuses would have had to be born, one of whom was kept under wraps for thirty-three years. Then, just when his brother underwent a painful, barbaric death, the twin brother would have had to come out of hiding so he could then come out as the resurrected Jesus—and, somehow, his body would be marred with identical and fresh crucifixion wounds!

This is conspiracy theory taken to the infinite power. It just doesn't make sense.

Mass Hallucination

With this theory, there is no doubt we have reached the apex of anti-resurrection theories. The mass hallucination theory implies that more than five hundred people must have had the same hallucination at the same time. According to Stedman's Medical Dictionary, the definition of "hallucination" is a false or distorted perception of objects or events with a compelling sense of their reality, usually resulting from a mental disorder or drug.[1]

During my years in medical practice, which includes my time in training in general surgery followed by a cardiothoracic fellowship and more than ten years as a practicing cardiac surgeon, I have seen patients hallucinating. Those patients hallucinate for several reasons. Sometimes we can find the reason, but other times we just can't. There is a trend in the hospitals to have private rooms, but semi-private rooms with two patients to a room are still very common. In all those years, I have never seen two patients in the same room having the same hallucination. In other words, I have never seen two patients having a coordinated perception of an object or event that does not exist except for in their minds. By its very definition, "hallucination" leaves no room for the possibility of two people perceiving the same event in the same way. Also keep in mind that there are different types of hallucinations: visual, auditory, olfactory, and others. The mass hallucination theory would require the achievement of an extremely complex hallucination in which five hundred people not only saw Jesus with their eyes, but also talked to him, listened to him, and touched him. It is medically impossible!

THE RESURRECTION—APOLOGETICS

Christians believe in the Resurrection largely by faith (including faith in the veracity of the biblical account). Believing in this extraordinary event proves to be a common denominator among Christians of every denomination. It is a paradox that the most difficult thing to believe is the one thing that all agree on.

Since the Resurrection has extraordinary implications for all of us, believers and nonbelievers, I would like to take some time to analyze it from an historical perspective.

History is a science. Here is a classic definition: "History is a narration of the events which have happened among mankind, including an account of the rise and fall of nations, as well as of other great changes which have affected the political and social condition of the human race."[2] It is based on documents that are organized following a methodology.

It has been established that Julius Caesar, Herod the Great, Herod Antipas, and Pontius Pilate were all real men and therefore part of human history. Jesus is also a historical figure. He did exist and he was a contemporary to them. One source of information is the New Testament of the Bible, in which five books describe Jesus' life and legacy: the four Gospels (Matthew, Mark, Luke, and John) and the Acts of the Apostles. Without contradicting each other, each one of these books documents the fact that Jesus Christ rose from the dead. We find differences in the narrative style of the five books, but they all say the same things concerning the Resurrection.

The issue of not having contradiction among the Gospels is very important. Human history is full of contradictions, depending a lot on an author's own perspective. If you read five different biographies of any single historical figure, you will find contradictions. Furthermore, while I have only cited the four Gospels included in the Bible, there are gospels not included in the Bible that also mention it. Now, some rationalists might argue that the Bible is a religious book and therefore biased. Yet the Bible contains historical data concerning Israel as a Roman colony that correlates with secular history books. The historical names mentioned earlier are examples of human beings who lived at the same time as Jesus, and their lives are also well-documented in other books. Therefore, it is safe to say that the Bible is historically accurate in terms of its portrayal of the time period, when Israel was a Roman colony.

We also should remember that the value of personal testimony is exclusively determined by the trustworthiness of the witness. Based on the testimony of the Bible, more than five hundred people stated that they had seen the resurrected Jesus (see 1 Corinthians 15:6). Some of those witnesses were later prosecuted, tortured, and even murdered for talking about it, but their testimony did not change. Who would become a martyr for a lie? People do not give up their lives for something they know is false.

Frank Morison, a rationalist lawyer and reporter, wrote a book titled *Who Moved the Stone?* This book was initially intended to disprove the Resurrection, and Morison believed that by doing so, he would be doing a great favor to humanity. He wanted to exhibit the real Jesus, whom he considered a great human being, a leader, but only a human. As a lawyer, he used his legal training to organize, evaluate, and categorize documentation. This process can be very tedious. I imagine him with four Bibles opened to different Gospels, comparing episode by episode, just looking for contradictions among them. He was looking for contradictions because contradiction is what weakens a testimony.

After this lawyer made a very detailed review of the information, he had to surrender his opinion—because of the consistency of the evidence.

The title of the first chapter of his book summarizes the drama of an investigator who slowly accepts the strength of the evidence: "The Book That Refused to be Written."[3] This honest rationalist author concludes his book with the following words: "There certainly is a deep and profoundly historical basis for that much disputed sentence in the Apostles' creed—'The third day He rose again from the dead.'"[4]

Look at the Evidence

Jesus' execution had a devastating effect on his followers. They became frightened and confused. Their leader was dead. The man that they had watched performing all kind of miracles had succumbed to death on the cross. He was not supposed to die. They had no idea what to do or where to go. Their dynamic experience with a charismatic Jesus was now only a memory.

How did they recover their enthusiasm and courage? What gave them the energy to relaunch a religious movement that in a relatively short time took over the whole Roman Empire and beyond? Only one event can explain this energy boost, and it is called "the Resurrection." They got to see him again. After he rose from the dead, he stayed around for forty days and then gave them their final instructions: "He said to them, 'Go into all the world and preach the gospel to all creation. Whoever believes and is baptized will be saved, but whoever does not believe will be condemned'" (Mark 16:15–16).

Before long, Christianity became the official religion of the Roman Empire, which meant that this new religious movement reached all the corners of the Empire and beyond. Obviously, dying on the cross did not limit Jesus' legacy. The physical death of Jesus did not stop what he started. The intimidation of the crucifixion did not work. Some of Jesus' followers were tortured, but no one gave up. We have been told that Peter got crucified head-down. It appears that Jesus' death boosted his religious movement. Let me rephrase that: the Resurrection boosted his religious movement.

While I was working on this manuscript, I decided to look for extrabiblical evidence of Jesus' resurrection. It was pleasantly surprising to discover that there is actual documentation of this event outside the Bible. A Jewish historian by the name of Flavius Josephus, who was a contemporary of Jesus and not a Christian, wrote at the end of the first century, in a work he called *Jewish Antiquities,* the following:

> Now there was about this time Jesus, a wise man, if it be lawful to call him a man; for he was a doer of wonderful works, a teacher of such men as receive the truth with pleasure. He drew over to him both many of the Jews and many of the Gentiles. He was [the] Christ. And when Pilate, at the suggestion of the principal men among us, had condemned him to the cross, those that loved him at the first did not forsake him; for he appeared to them alive again the third day, as the divine prophets of God had foretold these and ten thousand other wonderful things concerning him. And the tribe of the Christians, so named from him, are not extinct at this day.[5]

So we see that Jesus' resurrection is not just a religious myth based on faith. The resurrection is a historical event as documented by Josephus.

Earlier in this chapter we discussed the different rationalistic theories against the Resurrection. Every one of those theories was based on a fraud, a lie. Every theory represents a tight commitment to a lie. It is important to understand that time and details are the biggest enemies of a lie. Also, the more people that are involved in a fraud, the more difficult it is to keep it together.

Charles Colson, who was an assistant to President Nixon and involved in the Watergate scandal, learned in a profound way the repercussions of a fraud. This is a man who suffered the consequences of a lie that backfired, and here is what he has to say about the Resurrection:

> I know resurrection to be a fact, and Watergate proves me right. How? Because 12 men testified having seen Jesus rise from his

death, and then such truth was proclaimed for 40 years, without a single denial. Each one was beaten, tortured, stoned and imprisoned. They would have not been able to resist if it were not true. Watergate involved 12 of the most powerful men in the world—and they could not sustain a lie even for three weeks. Are you saying that 12 apostles could maintain a lie for a period of 40 years? Absolutely impossible. [6]

My initial goal with this book was to give some basic explanations about Jesus' suffering on the cross. I wanted to make the medical explanation of crucifixion understandable to everybody. In other words, what does a crucifixion do to a human body? By understanding the extraordinary suffering produced by the cross, and by realizing that Jesus could have avoided it, I wanted people to be able to acknowledge the real value of his sacrifice. Jesus' acceptance of the cross reveals his commitment to truth, righteousness, and nonviolence. He did not give up his ideals in order to avoid the outrageous death that lay ahead of him.

Other Biblical Resurrections

As I got deeper in the research, I also realized that Jesus' story is incomplete without the Resurrection. As I mentioned earlier, it is the Resurrection that sets him apart, otherwise he would be just another martyr in the history of mankind. Now Jesus' name is synonymous with resurrection. Any other cases of resurrection are related directly to Jesus—for example, the resurrection of Lazarus (see John 11:1–46) and the resurrection of the daughter of Jairus (see Mark 5:21–43). In both of them, the two dead people returned to life at the command of Jesus. Let's look at the resurrection of Lazarus:

> Then Jesus said, "Did I not tell you that if you believe, you will see the glory of God?"
> So they took away the stone. Then Jesus looked up and

said, "Father, I thank you that you have heard me. I knew that you always hear me, but I said this for the benefit of the people standing here, that they may believe that you sent me."

When he had said this, Jesus called in a loud voice, "Lazarus, come out!" The dead man came out, his hands and feet wrapped with strips of linen, and a cloth around his face.

Jesus said to them, "Take off the grave clothes and let him go."

JOHN 11:40–44

Jesus was making a strong statement with the resurrection of Lazarus. He wanted his disciples to have no doubts about his divine nature. It was very important that his disciples would have this episode fresh in their minds, since his crucifixion was coming and difficult days were ahead of them.

These scenarios do not portray the resuscitation maneuvers familiar to physicians and nurses. It is not about reestablishing circulation in somebody who just had a cardiac arrest and whose internal organs are still viable. Lazarus had been dead for four days. This is the real thing: coming back to life after having been buried.

The second case involves a twelve-year-old girl. Losing a youngster is never easy. It is not specified how long she had been dead, but most likely for a while, as the story reveals:

While Jesus was still speaking, some people came from the house of Jairus, the synagogue leader. "Your daughter is dead," they said. "Why bother the teacher anymore?"

Overhearing what they said, Jesus told him, "Don't be afraid; just believe."

He did not let anyone follow him except Peter, James and John the brother of James. When they came to the home of the synagogue leader, Jesus saw a commotion, with people crying and wailing loudly. He went in and said to them, "Why all this commotion and wailing? The child is not dead but asleep." But they laughed at him.

After he put them all out, he took the child's father and mother and the disciples who were with him, and went in where the child was. He took her by the hand and said to her, "Talitha koum!" (which means "Little girl, I say to you, get up!"). Immediately the girl stood up and began to walk around (she was twelve years old). At this they were completely astonished. He gave strict orders not to let anyone know about this, and told them to give her something to eat.

Mark 5:35–43

Jesus had again demonstrated that he had control over death. These two resurrection stories were the preamble to his.

Characteristics of Jesus' Resurrected Body

In a previous chapter I mentioned that the amount of information in the Bible can be overwhelming. There is such a variety of topics, from historical books to poetry. And last but not least, we have the Gospels and other books that present the life and legacy of Jesus. This is thousands of years condensed into one book. I have noticed how some parts go by unnoticed. I am not sure why certain episodes get my attention while others do not. It might be the combination of my physician's mind and my Christian faith.

As a Christian physician, I am very curious about Jesus' resurrected body. During my reading about the post-resurrection episodes, I found some fascinating features and unique details concerning his resurrected body. I would like to present my curiosity and my discoveries in an open way, realizing that all of it is truly beyond our human understanding. I find it very interesting.

After his resurrection, Jesus appeared to his disciples and friends multiple times. There are thirteen documented appearances and interactions of Jesus with his disciples. The Gospel of John suggests that there might have been more than thirteen.

One noticeable detail is that, for some reason, the disciples had some difficulty in the initial recognition of the resurrected Jesus. This particular difficulty is reported in all four Gospels. Let's review the encounter with Mary Magdalene, the first person to see him alive:

> He asked her, "Woman, why are you crying? Who is it you are looking for?"
>
> Thinking he was the gardener, she said, "Sir, if you have carried him away, tell me where you have put him, and I will get him."
>
> Jesus said to her, "Mary."
>
> She turned toward him and cried out in Aramaic, "Rabboni!" (which means "Teacher").
>
> Jesus said, "Do not hold on to me, for I have not yet ascended to the Father. Go instead to my brothers and tell them, 'I am ascending to my Father and your Father, to my God and your God.'"
>
> Mary Magdalene went to the disciples with the news: "I have seen the Lord!" And she told them that he had said these things to her.

JOHN 20:15–18

In this episode, Mary Magdalene thought that he was the gardener. It was early in the morning, just after sunset. She did not recognize him until he said "Mary." But also, for some reason, he said, "Do not hold on to Me, for I have not yet ascended to the Father." My impression is that Mary was going to give him a hug and he made that statement. The fact that he was not easily recognized and that he did not allow Mary to touch him so soon after his resurrection suggests that there must be something different and unique about the resurrected body. His statement suggests that he had to go through some process before anybody could touch him. We will see a different situation later when he does allow the disciples to touch him.

Later that day and still during daylight, two of his disciples were walking toward a nearby village called Emmaus. Jesus appeared to them and walked beside them for a while. The interaction between Jesus and the two disciples reflects also a significant difficulty in the initial recognition. Let's review the episode to better understand the encounter:

Now that same day two of them were going to a village called Emmaus, about seven miles from Jerusalem. They were talking with each other about everything that had happened. As they talked and discussed these things with each other, Jesus himself came up and walked along with them; but they were kept from recognizing him.

He asked them, "What are you discussing together as you walk along?"

They stood still, their faces downcast.

LUKE 24:13–17

These two disciples were deep in their conversation, sharing their feelings and emotions about the last few days. Again, a long conversation and interaction took place without Jesus being recognized. They walked together a considerable distance and even talked about the Scriptures, and yet they still didn't realize it was him. They finally realized his identity when Jesus broke the bread with them:

When he was at the table with them, he took bread, gave thanks, broke it and began to give it to them. Then their eyes were opened and they recognized him, and he disappeared from their sight. They asked each other, "Were not our hearts burning within us while he talked with us on the road and opened the Scriptures to us?"

LUKE 24:30–32

On the road to Emmaus, it is obvious that took a while for the disciples to identify Jesus. It is also noticeable that the word "disappeared" was used to explain how he left them. In reading other post-resurrection episodes we will find the words "appeared" and "disappeared" to describe Jesus' entrances and exits. Those particular words give a sense of supernaturalness. It's like describing a ghost, isn't it? Now, although I have never seen a ghost, our traditional understanding of what a ghost is like is that they do not have a solid component. Jesus' resurrected body was the same as before, but also radically different.

Before we continue analyzing Jesus' post-resurrection encounters, let's review what we have seen so far: (1) The difficulty in identifying Jesus during the daylight encounters; (2) He did not allow Mary to touch him soon after his resurrection; (3) He was able to appear and disappear; and (4) He was able to hold the bread, which implies that he was not just a vision like a hologram, or a ghost.

I have left the encounter with the ten disciples for last because Jesus himself clarified for his remaining disciples some issues about his post-resurrection body:

> While they were still talking about this, Jesus himself stood among them and said to them, "Peace be with you."
>
> They were startled and frightened, thinking they saw a ghost. He said to them, "Why are you troubled, and why do doubts rise in your minds? Look at my hands and my feet. It is I myself! Touch me and see; a ghost does not have flesh and bones, as you see I have."
>
> When he had said this, he showed them his hands and feet. And while they still did not believe it because of joy and amazement, he asked them, "Do you have anything here to eat?" They gave him a piece of broiled fish, and he took it and ate it in their presence.

LUKE 24:36–43

This episode occurred in a closed-door environment, in the upper room where the disciples were hiding, afraid of the authorities. This encounter occurred at evening, which is specified in John's version of the story. During this encounter, he was recognized immediately. I find this whole daylight versus evening difference very puzzling. During the daylight hours, people seemed to have difficulty recognizing him, but not at night. In his book *Who Moved the Stone,* Frank Morison also mentioned this particular and puzzling difficulty in recognizing the resurrected Jesus during the daylight. Here is what he had to say about it:

> There are signs in the Gospel that there may have been difficulties of a real and strictly scientific kind in establishing communication between what (for want of a more exact phrase) we must call the world of spirit and the world of sense. There is a certain quality in the *daylight* appearances that suggests that recognition was occasionally difficult, or, as a meteorologist would put it, the visibility was poor.
>
> But such parallels as we posses seem to indicate that darkness is favorable to certain delicate forms of transmission and reception. Do not even our wireless signals fade and recover as the twilight passes into the night?[7]

It is remarkable that Jesus did not knock and enter the regular way––through the door. He just materialized himself. The sudden appearance of Jesus among them scared the apostles. They thought they were seeing a ghost. This situation required Jesus to do some explaining to calm his friends down. This time, he allowed them to touch him, which is somewhat different from what he did with Mary Magdalene. Also, he ate with them. In other words, he made sure that they realized that he was not a ghost.

Now, by not using the front entrance, Jesus didn't make it easy for his disciples. When he just materialized between his friends, I can just imagine the disciples' reaction. Maybe because I am a Star Trek fan, I do find fascinating his ability to appear and disappear—not as an airy image but as a normal, solid body. It seems like the Bible is describing teleportation.

Jesus' appearance to the ten apostles (Thomas was missing) displays several unique characteristics: (1) teleportation—Jesus did not need to use doors anymore; (2) he had a body of flesh, so he was not a ghost—he was touchable; (3) his wounds remained in his resurrected body as proof of his sacrifice; and (4) it appeared as though as long as he was on earth, his body needed food, or, (another way to look at it) he was able to eat.

He was still fully human, because he had come back to life. Do you believe it, or are you a "doubting Thomas"?

After working on this book, I can see that the Resurrection is not just an event that we believe in because of our faith. It really happened. The question at this point shouldn't be whether or not Jesus did it, but rather *how* he did it. It is a fair question, but I don't expect any answers from science very soon.

The scientific and historical evidence in favor of the Resurrection is very solid. I find it very interesting that it was a nonbeliever who provided the most complete analysis in favor of the Resurrection. Frank Morison's efforts to demonstrate that Jesus didn't come back to life produced the opposite results. All of his careful research proved that Jesus did it—believe it or not.

Epilogue

I hope that reading this book has ignited some curiosity in you and stimulated you to learn more about Jesus. Even by learning more about Jesus as a human leader, you can get to know him as the Messiah. If you are a believer already, I hope that you have become more enthusiastic regarding the study of Jesus, the perfecter of our faith.

During the process of researching this book, I have learned that science and religion are not mutually exclusive. I discovered that superior intellectuals such as Louis Pasteur and Albert Einstein had a very profound faith in the living God. It's just a myth that scientists are not religious people, or that religious people are not scientists. While I started this book with the idea of learning more about the mechanism of death by crucifixion, that medical information became only part of the whole project. Each day, new avenues opened up and stimulated my curiosity. I read widely, and one of the greatest benefits was that I had to read the Bible. I always did read the Bible, but this time was different. This time, I was investigating. I was not just looking for a beautiful psalm that could help me on a bad day.

I found that, from the medical standpoint, the Bible provides great information that allows us to reconstruct Jesus' ordeal. The data is accurate historically, even down to small details. And the greatness of Jesus as a historical figure has no comparison. As a medical doctor and a Christian, I felt the need to reconcile two realities—faith and scientific facts—and they turned out not to be in conflict after all. So I have written about Jesus, his death and resurrection, out of my felt need to share my discoveries.

My career allows me to touch people's hearts physically. Now, through this book, I hope that God has touched yours. All the preparation and all the reading to write this book was fascinating, but at the end it only confirmed what I already knew, based on faith alone: *Jesus is the Messiah, the Son of God, and death has no power over him.* In the end, I found that the words of Saint Thomas Aquinas perfectly expressed my point of view:

> *To one who has faith, no explanation is necessary.*
> *To one without faith, no explanation is possible.*

NOTES

Chapter 1: The Shroud of Turin

1. Pierre Barbet, MD, *A Doctor at Calvary* (Fort Collins, CO: Roman Catholic Books, 1953), 17.
2. Ian Wilson, *The Blood and the Shroud* (New York, Free Press, 1998), 298.
3. Wilson, 300.
4. Barbet, 92–105.
5. Barbet, 105.
6. Wilson, 302.
7. Shroud of Turin website (www.shroud.com/78conclu.htm), summary of STURP's conclusions.
8. See "Pollen" on the Shroud of Turin blog (www.shroudstory.com) and Wilson, 303. See also Emanuela Marinelli, "The Question of Pollen Grains on the Shroud of Turin and the Sudarium of Oviedo," *Valencia*, April 28–30, 2012 (http://www.academia.edu/1536346/The_question_of_pollen_grains_on_the_Shroud_of_Turin_and_the_Sudarium_of_Oviedo).
9. Raymond N. Rogers, "Studies on the radiocarbon sample from the Shroud of Turin," *Thermochimica Acta* 425:1–2 (2005): 189–194.
10. Wilson, 88–89.
11. Shroud of Turin website (www.shroud.com/78conclu.htm), summary of STURP's conclusions.

Chapter 2: Historical Background

1. Goeffry Wawro, ed., *Historica: 1000 Years of Our Lives and Times* (Elanora Heights, NSW, Australia: Millennium House, 2006), 28.
2. Wawro, 26–30.
3. Olmedo, Jesús. *Jesús de Nazaret: Aproximación cordial, vivencial y creyente desde los pobres.* (Buenos Aires, Argentina: San Pablo, 2011), 50. See also Tom Wright, *The Original Jesus; The Life and Vision of a*

Revolutionary, (Grand Rapids, MI: Eerdmans, 1996), 27.

4. Olmedo, 48–54.

CHAPTER 3: JESUS CHRIST—THE MESSIAH

1. F.A. Larson, *The Star of Bethlehem* (www.bethlehemstar.net/the-day-of-the-cross/peters-argument. www.bethlehemstar.net/the-day-of-the-cross/the celestial dirge).

2. Colin Humphries, table, "Chronology of the Nativity."

3. David Hughes, table, "Published Chronology of the Nativity."

4. Mark R. Kidger, *The Star of Bethlehem: an Astromoner's View* (Princeton, NJ: Princeton University Press, 1960), 65.

5. Kidger, 66.

6. Bruce Chilton and Craig Evans, *Studying the Historical Jesus: Evaluations of the State of Current Research* (Leiden, The Netherlands: E.J. Brill, 1998), 124.

7. Chilton and Evans, 123–154.

8. James D.G. Dunn, *Jesus Remembered, Vol. 1* (Grand Rapids, MI: Eerdmans, 2003), 314–316.

9. Craig A. Evans, *Jesus and His World: the Archeological Evidence* (Louisville, KY: Westminster John Knox Press, 2012), 63–88.

10. Flavius Josephus, William Whiston, trans., *The New Complete Work of Josephus: Against Apion, book 1* (Grand Rapids, MI: Kregel Academic, 1999), 941.

11. Josephus, *Against Apion, book 2,* 973.

12. *The American Heritage Stedman's Medical Dictionary* (New York: Houghton Mifflin, 2001), 612.

CHAPTER 4: THE CRUCIFIXION

1. H.R. Jerajani, Bhagyashri Jaju, M.M. Phiske, and Nitin Lade. "Hematohidrosis: a Rare Clinical Phenomenon," *Indian Journal of Dermatology,* 54(3) (2009): 290–292.

2. Barbet, 48.

3. R. Lumpkin, "The Physical Suffering of Christ," *Journal of the Med-*

ical *Association of Alabama* 47 (1978): 8–10. David Terasaka, "Medical Aspects of the Crucifixion of Jesus Christ," *Blue Letter Bible* (2000), 1–18.

4. Dalya Alberge, "Study Shines Light on Final Steps of Christ," *Courier-Mail* (Brisbane, Australia), April 11, 2009 (archived at http://www.couriermail.com.au/news/pilgrims-on-wrong-path/story-e6frep26-1225699228574).

5. William D. Edwards, MD, Wesley J. Gabel, Floyd E. Hosmer, "The Physical Death of Jesus Christ," *Journal of the American Medical Association* 255(11)(1986): 1455–1463. (Reprinted at www.frugalsites.net/jesus/crucifixion.htm and at http://www.champs-of- truth.com/ lessons/tract_13g.htm.)

6. Terasaka.

7. Edwards, et al., Terasaka.

8. Barbet, 104.

9. Mark Eastman, MD, "Medical Aspects of the Crucifixion: the Agony of Love," reprinted on Koinonia House online (www.khouse.org/article/1998/113). Original published in the April 1998 *Personal Update News Journal.*

10. Edwards, et al.; Terasaka; Eastman.

11. Barbet, 113–127.

12. Larson. (www.bethlehemstar.net/the-day-of-the-cross/peters-argument. www.bethlehemstar.net/the-day-of-the-cross/the-celestial-dirge)

CHAPTER 5: THE RESURRECTION

1. *Stedman's Medical Dictionary,* 352.

2. John J. Anderson, *A Manual of General History* (New York: Clark & Maynard, 1876).

3. Frank Morison, *Who Moved the Stone?* (Grand Rapids, MI: Zondervan, 1958), 9.

4. Morison, 193.

5. Flavius Josephus, William Whiston, trans., *The New Complete Work*

of Josephus: Jewish Antiquities, book 18 (Grand Rapids, MI: Kregel Academic, 1999), 590.

6. Charles Colson, "The Paradox of Power," *Power to Change* (www.powertochange.ie/changed/index_Leaders)

BIBLIOGRAPHY

Anderson, John J. *A Manual of General History*. New York: Clark & Maynard. 1876.

Barbet, Pierre, MD. *A Doctor at Calvary*. Fort Collins, CO: Roman Catholic Books. 1953.

Baue, Arthur E., et al., eds. *Glenn's Thoracic and Cardiovascular Surgery*. Stamford, CT: Appleton & Lange. 1996.

Bulst, Wermer. *The Shroud of Turin*. Milwaukee, WI: Bruce Publishing Co. 1957.

Chilton, Bruce, and Craig Evans. *Studying the Historical Jesus: Evaluations of the State of Current Research*. Leiden, The Netherlands: E.J. Brill. 1998.

Dunn, James D.G. *Jesus Remembered, Vol. 1*. Grand Rapids, MI: Eerdmans. 2003.

Edwards, William D., Wesley J. Gabel, Floyd E. Hosmer. "The Physical Death of Jesus Christ." *Journal of the American Medical Association* 255(11)(1986): 1455–1463.

Evans, Craig A. *Jesus and His World: The Archaeological Evidence*. Louisville, KY: Westminster John Knox. 2012.

Jerajani, H.R., Bhagyashri Jaju, M.M. Phiske, and Nitin Lade. "Hematohidrosis: a Rare Clinical Phenomenon," *Indian Journal of Dermatology,* 54(3) (2009).

Josephus, Flavius, William Whiston, trans., *The New Complete Work of Josephus*. Grand Rapids, MI: Kregel. 1999.

Kidger, Mark. R. *The Star of Bethlehem: An Astronomer's View*. Princeton, NJ: Princeton University Press. 1960.

Lumpkin, R. "The physical suffering of Christ," *Journal of the Medical Association of Alabama* 47 (1978), 8–10.

Miller, Thomas A, and B.J. Rowland, eds. *The Physiologic Basis of Modern Surgical Care*. Washington, DC: C.V. Mosby. 1988.

Morison, Frank. *Who Moved the Stone?* Grand Rapids, MI: Zondervan. 1958.

Nyhus, Lloyd M., Josef E. Fischer, Robert J. Baker, eds. *Mastery of Surgery.* Boston: Little, Brown. 1992.

Olmedo, Jesús. *Jesús de Nazaret: Aproximación cordial, vivencial y creyente desde los pobres.* Buenos Aires, Argentina. San Pablo. 2011.

Rogers, Raymond N. "Studies on the Radiocarbon Sample from the Shroud of Turin," *Thermochimica Acta* 425:1–2 (2005).

Sabiston, David C., MD. *The Biological Basis of Modern Surgical Practice.* Philadelphia: W.B. Saunders. 1991.

Schwartz, Seymour I., MD. *Principles of Surgery.* New York: McGraw-Hill. 1994.

Wawro, Goeffry, ed., *Historica: 1000 Years of Our Lives and Times.* Elanora Heights, NSW, Australia: Millennium House. 2006.

Wilson, Ian. *The Blood and the Shroud.* New York: Free Press. 1998.

Wright, Tom (N.T.). *The Original Jesus: The Life and Vision of a Revolutionary.* Grand Rapids, MI: Eerdmans. 1996.

---

[*] This same story appears in Mark 14:12–26; Luke 22:7–23; John 13:21–26.

Please visit: www.josejnorbertobooks.com

Facebook: @josejnorbertobooks